GREAT LIVES OBSERVED

Gerald Emanuel Stearn, *General Editor*

EACH VOLUME IN THE SERIES VIEWS THE CHARACTER AND ACHIEVEMENT OF A GREAT WORLD FIGURE IN THREE PERSPECTIVES—THROUGH HIS OWN WORDS, THROUGH THE OPINIONS OF HIS CONTEMPORARIES, AND THROUGH RETROSPECTIVE JUDGMENTS—THUS COMBINING THE INTIMACY OF AUTOBIOGRAPHY, THE IMMEDIACY OF EYEWITNESS OBSERVATION, AND THE OBJECTIVITY OF MODERN SCHOLARSHIP.

MAURICE ASHLEY, *the editor of this volume in the Great Lives Observed series, is Research Fellow in the Department of Social Studies and Economics at Loughborough University of Technology and the President of the Cromwell Association. He is also the author of* The Greatness of Oliver Cromwell, Oliver Cromwell and the Puritan Revolution, The Financial and Commercial Policy of the Cromwellian Protectorate, *and* Cromwell's Generals.

GREAT LIVES OBSERVED

Cromwell

Edited by MAURICE ASHLEY

*It is from his own words, as I have ventured
to believe, from his own Letters and
Speeches well read, that the world may first
obtain some dim glimpse of the actual Cromwell,
and see him darkly face to face. What little
is otherwise ascertainable, cleared from
the circumambient inanity and insanity,
may be stated in brief compass.*

—THOMAS CARLYLE

A SPECTRUM BOOK

PRENTICE-HALL, INC., ENGLEWOOD CLIFFS, N.J.

Preface

As the first aim of this book is exposition, I have ventured to modernize most of the punctuation and capitalization in the seventeenth-century documents; and I have not in all cases, though I have in some, gone to the originals, but have relied on modern editions. In fact what is badly needed is a fresh scholarly edition of Cromwell's speeches and correspondence, which should include new material discovered in recent years.

I have to acknowledge no help in the preparation of this book; it has been done in sweat and blood on my own typewriter. But as I have devoted much of my life to a study of this great man, I hope it will serve.

Contents

PART ONE
CROMWELL LOOKS AT THE WORLD

1
The Chain of Providence   12

Conversion, *12*   "He Will Be Speaking in Your Ear,"
13   "He That Ruleth Over Men Must Be Just, Ruling
in the Fear of God," *15*   Religion the Cause of the
Civil War, *17*

2
Negotiation Preferable to Coercion   19

"Whatsoever We Get by a Treaty Will Be Firm and
Durable," *19*   "Not Wedded and Glued to Forms of
Government," *21*   "The Face of Authority," *23*   "We
Wait Upon the Lord," *25*

3
The Execution of the King   27

"Impartial Justice," *27*   "Exemplary Justice," *28*   Casting Off Tyranny, *28*   In Answer to Their Consciences,
28

PART THREE
CROMWELL IN HISTORY

GREAT LIVES OBSERVED

CROMWELL

Introduction

Oliver Cromwell was a conservative, in that he believed in upholding established institutions such as Parliament and the rule of law; he was a radical, in that he was convinced that particular laws needed reforming (and that lawyers often were interested parties wishing to maintain slow and expensive procedures); he was a liberal, because he passionately believed in the freedom of the mind, in the right of every man to work out the truth for himself; and above all, he was a Christian, devoting his life to the service of God and the godly people within the British Commonwealth, as he understood them.

Historians sometimes have gone wrong about Cromwell, for—as often is the case when they delineate great men—they have been tempted to oversimplify him, calling him a conservative *or* a radical *or* a libertarian *or* a Christian fanatic. He was all of these, but not any one of them alone. Men's thoughts and outlooks are composed of many strands. The Marxist notion that men invariably reflect the point of view and aspirations of the class into which they happen to be born is one that I reject not merely as unscientific but as contrary to all my experiences in life. Freud was much nearer the mark in suggesting that most men and women, at least when they are young, are moved by personal emotions deeply burning within them. To dismiss Cromwell as a resentful or hopeful country gentleman from the backwoods or the back benches is too easy. Men can be, and have been, motivated by a conscious sense of duty. And Cromwell was aware of duty both to God and to his country. He objected to the view that men are born to pleasure or to satisfy their own personal desires or aspirations. Life, he was convinced, had a meaning and a purpose; men were intended to serve a cause other than their own.

Of course, Oliver Cromwell was ambitious; but, as I have written elsewhere, ambition is merely the driving force that impels men onward in their path through life, if they are not morons or yes-

1

men or other-directed, to employ a once fashionable sociological phrase. All the great figures in history have felt that they were able to serve their cause or their country better than anyone else could. In the same way, authors believe they can write better books than other authors.

But fundamentally, Cromwell was a modest man. Only gradually, and when he already had reached middle age, did he realize that he possessed the rare and indefinable gift of leadership. Like most natural leaders, he did not reach decisions rapidly, though occasionally he was carried away by his temper, as when, for example, he dissolved his last Protectorate Parliament. One asks whether he made the wisest use of his powers of leadership and whether, if some other man had become the guiding star in the Puritan republic, events would have developed differently. Would a John Pym or a John Eliot, a Hampden or an Ireton—all of them men who died before the Cromwellian Protectorate was established—have directed the British Commonwealth along some other course than that which led to a supreme moment of triumph for Nonconformist ideals and then inevitably, as it has seemed to historians, to the restoration of the old regime under Charles II? My own feeling is that their rule might have been much more rigid and that the crash would have come sooner.

Possibly what the world today remembers about Oliver Cromwell is, first, that he was the leader of the Roundhead army in the English civil war that resulted in the overthrow of the Stuart monarchy; secondly, that he was responsible for the execution of Charles I, who died in 1649 on a scaffold before a silent crowd at Whitehall; and lastly, that Cromwell was the general who in an outburst of sadistic cruelty ordered the extermination of the garrison of Drogheda, in Ireland, after it had gallantly defended the town. None of these things is true, or at least entirely true; history rarely is as simple as that. To begin with, Cromwell was not the leader of the Roundhead army at any time until the campaign in Scotland in 1650. The commander-in-chief of the New Model Army, which was formed after the aristocratic Earl of Essex proved himself an incompetent general, was Thomas Fairfax, a Yorkshireman who eventually welcomed the restoration of the Stuarts and whose wife staged a demonstration of protest during the trial of

Charles I. Admittedly, Cromwell distinguished himself as a commander in the eastern part of England at the outset of the war and played a prominent part in Parliamentarian victories at Marston Moor and Naseby. But it was Fairfax who was responsible for the organization of the New Model Army, and it was John Pym who was the prime organizer of victory and whose efforts brought in the Scots to turn the scale against the Royalists in England.

As to the trial and execution of the King, Oliver Cromwell long hesitated over so drastic and terrible a course. The original impulse appears to have come from his austere son-in-law, Henry Ireton, and the officers of the southern half of the Parliamentarian army, who were infuriated when the Royalists, defeated in the first civil war and having given their word of honor not to fight again, were inspired by their master to rekindle the flames of strife in 1648 and to arouse Kent and Essex once more to battle. When Cromwell was returning from the northern campaign in which he stopped the Scottish "Engagers" whom Charles I had invited into England, he received the news of the southern army's demand for the trial of the King. He remained in Yorkshire while he made up his mind what to do. There is evidence that even when he returned to London, he still hoped to save the King's life. During 1647, Cromwell had attempted to come to terms with the King and to reconcile him with Parliament and the Roundhead army. Also, later on, he contemplated allowing the King's youngest son to succeed to the throne under Parliament's auspices. In no sense was Cromwell ever a rigid republican or anti-monarchist and he was deeply moved by Charles's plight as a man and as a father, though he had come, with good reason, to distrust him as a statesman. But when Cromwell finally made up his mind that the King must be tried, he recognized that justice would have to be executed upon him as a "man of blood" who had wilfully provoked the second war and broken his word of honor. Thus, in the end, in company with a group of determined revolutionaries, Cromwell pushed through the King's trial and execution.

With regard to the episode at Drogheda, I have argued strongly elsewhere that this certainly was the result not of any sadistic outburst on Cromwell's part, but of a deliberate military decision. Since invariably I have been asked about it when addressing American and other audiences on Cromwell, I will summarize the argument as briefly as I can. When Cromwell landed in Ireland in 1649, the country still was largely under the control of his enemies, and he led his expeditionary force into hostile territory where guerrilla warfare and stubborn sieges easily might have hampered the movements of his army and bogged it down during the winter. The Royalist garrison of Drogheda consisted of some two or three thousand men when they were assaulted by a much superior army. Once a breach had been blown in the walls of the town, the position of the garrison became hopeless; the best it could do was to inflict delaying casualties upon the assaulting force. The laws of war in those days permitted the refusal of quarter to a garrison that stood an assault after rejecting a summons. The great Duke of Wellington declared in 1820 that this refusal was "not a useless effusion of blood." Cromwell himself said afterwards, "Truly I believe this bitterness will save much effusion of blood" and "will tend to prevent effusion of blood in the future." In fact some of the garrison escaped, and some had their lives spared. As a result of this slaughter of most of the garrison of Drogheda, a number of other Irish towns surrendered to the English without fighting, and many lives on both sides must have been saved. Cromwell himself accepted the view that the refusal of quarter always brought remorse and could be justified only as a deliberate act of war.

Among Cromwell's most notable contributions to British history, which are acknowledged by almost all historians, is, first, his establishing in England, Scotland, and Ireland a period of peace after nearly ten years of civil war. "He fought to end our fighting," wrote a contemporary poet. Probably no one else in his time could have achieved so much, for soon after his death anarchy broke loose. But the Cromwellian Protectorate had afforded the British people an interval of comparative prosperity and internal peace.

Secondly, Cromwell made England into a great power, feared and admired by her European neighbors. This was freely admitted by such Royalists as the first Earl of Clarendon and Samuel Pepys the diarist, who has been described as the savior of the Royal Navy. Cromwell had a gift for selecting able generals and admirals, some of whom served Charles II after his restoration. General Monck was an effective ruler of Scotland. Sir John Reynolds successfully commanded a British expeditionary force when Great Britain entered into an alliance with France. Robert Blake was an outstanding fighting man at sea who inflicted defeats upon the Spaniards and suppressed the pirates in the Mediterranean. Cromwell befriended Charles X of Sweden, came to terms with the Dutch republicans, gained Jamaica (later a prosperous colony), and acquired Dunkirk in Flanders, which until then had been a nest of pirates and a thorn in the flesh of British merchant seamen. When Charles II and James II reigned, British prestige abroad declined. At one time, the navy was so neglected that the Dutch fleet was able to sail into the Medway and attack Chatham. The British standing army showed no sense of loyalty to James II. In fact, it was not until the second son of Charles I had been ousted from his throne by his own son-in-law, Prince William of Orange, that Great Britain once more became a leading European power.

Cromwell's third remarkable achievement was to establish Nonconformity so firmly in England that it remained a fundamental and influential part of the British way of life for at least another three hundred years. He honestly believed in liberty of conscience for all his fellow Christians, provided it was compatible with the maintenance of law and order. There was, admittedly, a duality in his outlook. Being an Independent, or Congregationalist, he believed in the right of congregations to choose their own ministers and in the maintenance of an ordered system in the churches. Thus, he could not approve of the acts of extreme sects like the Quakers, or Society of Friends, and the Fifth Monarchy Men in breaking up church services and shouting ministers down from their pulpits. This emerges clearly from the conversations (from which I print extracts) he had with George Fox, the founder of the Society of Friends, and John Rogers, one of the chief preachers among the Fifth Monarchy Men. Nevertheless, he tried to understand their point of view and to persuade them that if they would be content to preach their gospel in a peaceable manner, his government would leave them alone. Similarly, he attempted to induce John Lilburne, the leader of the Levelers, a political group that advocated radical ideas, that if he would only promise to refrain from stirring up mutiny in the army, he would be allowed to propagate his views, however distasteful they might be to conservatives.

It sometimes is argued that it is absurd to speak of Cromwell as a libertarian, when he would not tolerate two of the most powerful brands of the Christian religion—Roman Catholicism and Anglicanism, or Episcopalianism. To the Irish he denied the right to celebrate the Mass. Like many Protestant Englishmen of his time, he had a blind spot where Irish Catholicism was concerned and evidently regarded the Mass as a superstitious practice inspiring revolutionary and bloodthirsty Irishmen. But this much may be said. In England, during the Protectorate, he did not interfere with Roman Catholics' celebrating the Mass in their private houses, which was as much freedom (except at the royal court, where there had been two Roman Catholic Queens) as he had been allowed under the first two Stuart monarchs. In a famous letter written to Cardinal Mazarin, the effective head of the French Government, Cromwell maintained that the Roman Catholics in England were better off under his Protectorate than they had been before; and in fact, the French representative in London confirmed this. Again, as to the Anglicans, during the Protectorate there was little interference with the use of the Book of Common Prayer at private services. The American historian Robert Bosher wrote, "There is good evidence that the government's policy [during the years after Cromwell became Lord Protector] sought to move beyond a limited indulgence of Anglicans." Cromwell opened negotiations with the Bishop of Exeter as early as 1652. In 1654, a Northamptonshire squire wrote, "The news is very current about the town that the Protector expressed thus much that the ministry should discreetly use the Common Prayer; I hear this from persons of great credit." And Professor W. K. Jordan observed that "in numerous rural counties ministers conducted the traditional services through the period without molestation."

In relation to the Church of England, most of whose leading members were Royalists, the main difficulty was the episcopacy, which had been officially abolished by Parliament and the Bishop's properties sold. Under Charles I, many members of the parliaments and many people throughout the nation, as Dr. Christopher Hill has shown, deeply resented the secular powers of the old Church, whether exercised by the Bishops or by other ecclesiastical authorities. And these powers were never in fact restored in full. Recently, it has been persuasively argued that the so-called English Presbyterian movement largely consisted of Low-Church Anglicans, and that Charles I knew this when he was prepared to make concessions to the Presbyterians as the price for his restoration to the throne. It was thought that English Presbyterianism might easily merge into a mild form of Episcopalianism, such as had existed for a spell under James VI in Scotland. When one of the principal Presbyterian leaders, Richard Baxter, was offered a bishopric after the Restoration, this therefore lay in the logic of history; and undoubtedly many English Presbyterians returned eventually to the bosom of the established Church. Moreover, Cromwell himself accepted the need for maintaining an established Church—though giving rather more freedom to congregations to choose their own ministers and preachers—and even for paying for this Church by means of the much hated tithe until a better system could be devised. Outside the framework of the national Church, Cromwell was ready to tolerate and protect all the sects, provided they behaved themselves within the context of law and order. He also took the first steps that enabled a Jewish community to dwell openly in England. Cromwell may have been, as once was said, a "spiritual anarchist," but he did not favor anarchy in the Church. It is high time the religious history of the Protectorate was rewritten.

No one who reads Cromwell's letters and speeches in an impartial frame of mind can fail to appreciate that he believed passionately in the freedom of the mind and the liberty of the spirit. As Ernest Barker wrote more than thirty years ago (see page 151), this belief imperceptibly merged into a wider concept of freedom. No one can doubt, after reading what he said, where Cromwell would have stood on the racial issue today.

It sometimes is asserted that Cromwell was in no sense a constructive statesman, that he was a destroyer rather than a builder, and that no traces of his work remained after the Restoration in 1660. Understandably, the restored Royalists were unwilling to confess that they owed anything at all to Cromwell. But in fact, a number of constitutional changes were preserved, the law courts were to some extent reformed (English became their language), and the navigation acts for upholding British shipping and shipbuilding, which had been strengthened during the Interregnum, were re-enacted in the reign of Charles II. But to study Cromwell's own ideas, one needs to read through the eighty-two ordinances approved by him and his Council of State between the time when the Protectorate was set up under the constitution known as "the Instrument of Government" and the time when the first Protectorate parliament was called. The two Protectorate parliaments were not greatly interested in legislation, for they regarded themselves as constituent assemblies entitled to revise, or modify, the new form of government. Cromwell, on the other hand, thought that the political revolution that had been completed, symbolized by the execution of King Charles, should be the prelude to the reform of the laws and the "reformation of manners." And he himself took an active part in urging the need to reform the law—in particular to abolish the death penalty for minor offenses and to secure the release of thousands of poor debtors from imprisonment. Also, he was, of course, a Puritan who aimed to suppress drunkenness, swearing, and adultery, though not by using the extreme penalties that some of his fellow Puritans wanted imposed. His own hobbies were horses and music and, on the whole, like most sensible men, he grew more tolerant toward the younger generation as he became older.

Recently, it has been forcibly argued that Cromwell's policy was to uplift the class from which he himself sprang—the middle class, the country gentry. Though in the end, he tried to construct a House of Lords of his own choosing, selected from the godly people of the land, he disliked the influence of the old nobility both in England and in Scotland, much as during his youth, he had taken part in the struggle to destroy the power of the Church of England Bishops. It is understandable why Cromwell was so much admired by the late Victorians, men like Gardiner or Morley; for in a way, the kind of reforms for which he contended resembled the legal reforms advocated by Charles Dickens, the religious equality sought by the Nonconformists, and the maintenance of traditional middle-class family life in which they themselves believed. Much water has flowed under the bridges not merely since Cromwell ruled over England, but also since Mr. Gladstone did. Therefore it is not easy for us to appreciate what Mr. Trevor-Roper has called

Cromwell's policy of "laicization" and "decentralization," for we live in a world whose attitudes toward religion and morality are different and in which central governments more and more have taken over the administration of public welfare and education—and even morality.

For this book, I have chosen passages both from Cromwell's own letters and speeches (modernizing the punctuation and spelling as much as I can) and from writings by contemporaries and by historians, to illustrate how differently from ourselves he looked at things and to show how different people have looked at him. It is necessary to read such extracts with care and not to take them all at their face value. Cromwell was not a philosopher or even a political thinker and he addressed himself to a variety of audiences, struggling both to explain himself and to understand them. During the Enlightenment, in the eighteenth century, he generally was regarded as a hypocrite and a liar. The twentieth century, more scientifically, has tried to fit him into some Marxist or sociological pattern. In studying a great life, we have to make up our own minds about what was most significant in the man's career. In this introduction, I have tried to indicate briefly what I regard as important in Cromwell's career. But I hope that readers may be induced by this book to interest themselves further in the subject and to widen their range of study, thus becoming able to reach their own conclusions about this very remarkable man.

Chronology of the Life of Cromwell

1599	(April 25) Born at Huntingdon; son of Robert Cromwell and Elizabeth Steward.
1616	Admitted a Fellow Commoner of Sidney Sussex College, Cambridge.
1620	Marries Elizabeth Bourchier, daughter of a City merchant, at St. Giles's church, Cripplegate, in London.
1628	Elected member of Parliament for his native borough of Huntingdon.
1636	Inherits property from uncle and settles in Ely, where he lives until 1647.
1640	Elected member of Parliament for borough of Cambridge.
1642	Raises a troop of cavalry to fight in first civil war.
1643	Becomes colonel of cavalry regiment and takes part in campaign against Royalists in eastern England.
1644	Is appointed Lieutenant-General under the Earl of Manchester and distinguishes himself in the battle of Marston Moor. In House of Commons, criticizes conduct of war and advocates "Self-Denying Ordinance" depriving members of Parliament of army commands.
1645	In spite of "Self-Denying Ordinance," becomes Lieutenant-General in Sir Thomas Fairfax's "New Model Army." Takes command of right wing at battle of Naseby.
1646	Is voted £2,500 a year by Parliament as reward for military services.
1647	After vainly trying to reconcile Parliament and the New Model Army, throws in his lot with the army, approves seizure of King by army, and marches into London with army to overawe Parliament. Takes chair at army debates about future settlement of kingdom.
1648	Takes command in Wales and then in northern England during civil war. Wins battle of Preston and leads army into Scotland.
1649	(January) Takes part in trial of Charles I and signs death warrant. (August) Leads expeditionary force to Ireland.

10

1650	Defeats Scottish Covenanters at battle of Dunbar.
1651	Defeats Charles II at battle of Worcester.
1653	(April) Cromwell expels the "Rump" of the Long Parliament, which had sat since 1640. (July) Addresses "Assembly of Saints" nominated and summoned by Council of Army Officers. (December 12) Cromwell becomes Lord Protector of England, Scotland, and Ireland.
1654	(September 3) Cromwell addresses first Protectorate parliament.
1655	(January) Dismisses first Protectorate parliament. (May) Institutes system of Major-Generals of Horse Militia to reinforce local government. Force sent by Cromwell to West Indies occupies Jamaica. (October) Is involved in war against Spain.
1656	(Septmber) Meets second Protectorate parliament.
1657	(March) Signs offensive alliance with France. (May) Cromwell refuses offer of Crown by Parliament.
1658	(February) Cromwell dismisses second Protectorate parliament. (June) British troops take part in battle of the Dunes, and Dunkirk is handed over to Cromwell's government. (September 3) Cromwell dies in Whitehall Palace.

PART ONE

CROMWELL LOOKS AT THE WORLD

1

The Chain of Providence

And what are all our histories and other traditions of actions in former times but God manifesting Himself?

Cromwell, January 22, 1655.

Oliver Cromwell was essentially a man of action; to understand his outlook on the world, we have to dig deeply into the meaning of his speeches and correspondence. Moreover, no one can possibly hope to understand him without appreciating the fact that he was a convinced Christian, who believed that what was done in the world revealed a purpose and a design. He underwent the experience of conversion, which was common among Puritans, comparatively late in life, when he was a married man of twenty-eight with five children. He came to believe that his victories in war, over both his domestic and his foreign enemies, signified God's wishes. These were "dispensations" that needed to be marked and assessed. Yet they were not always easy to detect, and it might be possible to be mistaken about them or to make too much of them. But on the whole, he thought that he could understand them. "If thou wilt seek to know the will of God in all that chain of Providence," he once wrote, "seek of the Lord to teach thee what it is; and He will do it."

CONVERSION

In one of his earliest surviving letters, written to a woman cousin on October 13, 1638, Cromwell describes his conversion.

I thankfully acknowledge your love in your kind remembrance of me upon this opportunity. Alas, you do too highly prize my lines and my company. I may be ashamed to own your expressions, considering how unprofitable I am, and the mean improvement of my talent.

Yet to honour God by declaring what He hath done for my soul, in this I am confident, and I will be so. Truly, then, this I find: that He giveth springs in a dry and barren wilderness where no water is. I live (you know where) in Mesheck, which they say signifies Prolonging; in Kedar, which signifieth Blackness: yet the Lord forsaketh me not. Though He do prolong, yet He will (I trust) bring me to His tabernacle, to His resting-place. My soul is with the congregation of the first-born, my body rests in hope, and if here I may honour my God either by doing or by suffering, I shall be most glad.

Truly no creature hath more cause to put forth himself in the cause of his God than I. I have had plentiful wages beforehand and I am sure I shall never earn the least mite. The Lord accept me in His Son and give me to walk in the light. He it is that enlighteneth our blackness, our darkness. I dare not say: He hideth His face from me. He giveth me to see light in His light. One beam in a dark place hath exceeding much refreshment in it. Blessed be His name for shining upon so dark a heart as mine! You know what my manner of life hath been. Oh, I lived in and loved darkness and hated the light: I was a chief, the chief of sinners. This is true: I hated godliness, yet God had mercy on me. Oh the riches of His mercy! Praise Him for me, pray for me, that He who hath begun a good work would perfect it to the day of Christ.

"HE WILL BE SPEAKING IN YOUR EAR"

Under the doctrine of the omnipresence of God, it becomes essential for all men and women who are conscious that with their conversion they become Chosen People to seek to understand God's wishes, to lead an upright and dedicated life— whether in private or in public—and to bear witness to their faith. Cromwell constantly reminded his family of this, as in these extracts from two of his letters, one written to his eldest daughter Bridget and the other to Dorothy, the wife of the elder of the two sons who survived him.

Your sister [Elizabeth] is (I trust in mercy) exercised with some perplexed thoughts. She seeks her own vanity and carnal mind, bewailing it: she seeks after (as I hope also) that which will satisfy. And thus to be a seeker is to be of the best sect next to a finder; and such an one shall every faithful humble seeker be at the end. Happy seeker, happy finder! Who ever tasted that the Lord is gracious without some sense of self, vanity and badness? Who ever tasted that graciousness of His and could go less in desire and less than pressing after full enjoyment? Dear heart, press on; let not husband, let not anything cool thy affections after Christ. I hope he will be an occasion to inflame them. That which is best worthy of love in thy husband is that of the image of Christ he bears. Look on that and love it best, and all the rest for that. I pray for thee and him; do so for me.[1]

I desire you both to make it above all things your business to seek the Lord: to be frequently calling upon Him that He would manifest Himself to you in His Son, and be listening what returns He makes to you, for He will be speaking in your ear and in your heart, if you attend thereunto. I desire you provoke your husband likewise thereunto. As for the pleasures of this life and outward business, let that be upon the bye. Be above all these things by faith in Christ and then you shall have the true use and comfort of them, and not otherwise. I have much satisfaction in hope your spirit is this way set, and I desire you may grow in grace and in the knowledge of our Lord and Saviour Jesus Christ, and that I may hear thereof. The Lord is very near, which we see by His wonderful works, and therefore He looks that we of this generation draw near to Him. This late mercy of Ireland [the defeat of the Royalist Duke of Ormonde at Rathmines near Dublin] is a great manifestation thereof.[2]

[1] Letter of October 25, 1642.
[2] To Mrs. Richard Cromwell, August 22, 1649.

"HE THAT RULETH OVER MEN MUST BE JUST, RULING IN THE FEAR OF GOD" [3]

Consistently with his providential view of life, Cromwell believed that God called men to serve him and that those who ruled the country must do so in a Christian spirit and in accordance with God's will. To fulfil this aim, Cromwell, as commander-in-chief, and his officers first tried to set up a government of their own chosen people to replace both the Stuart monarchy and the "Rump" of the Long Parliament, whose members they said included drunkards, whoremasters, and "jugglers." They therefore nominated what came to be known as the Assembly of Saints, in which they had high hopes, though in fact it later disappointed them by its inability to govern. In addressing this Assembly, Cromwell told the members that they had come through "strivings" and "blood" by their victories over the English Royalists and the Scottish Covenanters and had been elected by God, not men, to undertake "the supreme authority of this nation." This was the spirit in which he welcomed them to their duties:

Truly God hath called you to this work by, I think, as wonderful providences as ever passed upon the sons of men in so short a time. And truly, I think, taking the argument of necessity, for the government must not fall. Taking the appearance of God in this thing, I am sure you would have been loath it should have been resigned into the hands of wicked men and enemies. I am sure God would not have it so. It's come therefore to you by way of necessity, by the way of the wise providence of God—though through weak hands. And therefore, I think, coming through our hands, though such as we are, it may not be taken ill if we do offer somewhat . . . to the discharge of the trust which is incumbent upon you. And although I seem to speak of that which may have the face and interpretation of a change, it's a very humble one: and if he that means to be a servant to you, who hath now

[8] Speech of July 4, 1653.

called you to the exercise of the supreme authority, discharge that which he conceives to be a duty to you, we hope you will take it in good part.

And truly I shall not hold you long in it; because I hope it's written in your hearts to approve yourselves to God. Only this Scripture I shall remember to you, which hath been much upon my spirit: in Hosea, xi, 12: "Judah yet ruleth with God and is faithful with the Saints." It's said before that "Ephraim compassed God about with lies and the house of Israel with deceit." How God hath been compassed about by fastings and thanksgivings and other exercises and transactions, I think we have cause to lament. Truly you are called by God to rule with Him and for Him. And you are called to be faithful with the Saints who have been somewhat instrumental to your call. Second Samuel, xxi, 3: "He that ruleth over men", the Scripture saith, "must be just, ruling in the fear of God."

And truly it's better for [us] to pray for you than to counsel you in that matter that you may exercise the judgment of mercy and truth. It's better, I say, to pray for you than to counsel you; to ask wisdom from Heaven for you; which I am confident many thousands of saints do this day, and have done, and will do, through the permission of God and His assistance. I say it's better to pray than advise; yet truly I think of another Scripture, which is very useful, though it seems to be for common application to every man as a Christian—wherein he is counselled to ask wisdom; and he is told what that wisdom is that's from above. It's "pure, peaceable, gentle and easy to be entreated, full of mercy and good fruits; it's "without partiality and without hypocrisy." Truly my thoughts run much upon this place that to the execution of judgment (the judgment of truth, for that's the judgment) you must have wisdom from above, and that's pure. That will teach you to exercise the judgment of truth; it's without partiality. Purity, impartiality, sincerity—these are the effects of wisdom and these will help you to exercise the judgment of truth. And then if God give you the hearts to be easy to be entreated, to be peaceably spirited, to be full of good fruits, bearing good fruits to the nation, to men as men, to the people of God, to all in their several stations—this will teach you to execute the judgment of mercy and truth. And I have little more to say to this. I shall rather bend my prayers for you in that behalf, as I said; and many others will.

RELIGION THE CAUSE OF THE CIVIL WAR [4]

Though Cromwell believed that he and his fellow Puritans had been called by God to govern the three nations of England, Scotland, and Ireland, he thought that the cause of the civil war was that the monarchy and the Church of England had refused to allow Christians to find God and to interpret his wishes by their own means—through prayer, with the aid of teachers of their own choosing, and by the study of the Bible. Cromwell did not think that any arbitrarily appointed hierarchy should prescribe how men and women were to seek God and study his wishes. He strove for individual freedom and believed that neither the Pope, as Bishop of Rome, nor the English Bishops could order men's personal religion. Images, ceremonies, and the Mass he regarded alike as relics of discarded superstitions. Men must seek and find God for themselves. That was the basic liberty. That was why in his very first speech in the House of Commons, he attacked a clergyman who preached "flat popery" and was upheld against his critics by the Bishop of Winchester. In the Long Parliament, which met in 1640, he showed himself uncompromisingly hostile to the authorities who ruled the Church of England, because he believed that they were reviving "popery" and preventing the free discussion of Christianity. He demonstrated his animosity against the bishops by advocating the abolition of their offices as well as of their secular powers, and he stood ready to fight against the monarchy because it was sustaining "the tyranny of the bishops." The immediate cause of the war, however, had been Parliament's refusal to allow a King it had come to mistrust to retain control of the militia, the only armed force in the kingdom.

Religion was not the first thing contested for, but God brought it to that issue at last; and gave it unto us by way of redundancy; and at last it proved that which was most dear to us. And wherein

[4] Speech of January 22, 1655.

consisted this more than in obtaining that liberty from the tyranny of the bishops to all species of Protestants to worship God according to their own light and consciences, for want of which many of our brethren forsook their native countries to seek their bread from strangers and to live in howling wildernesses; and for which also many that remained here were imprisoned and otherwise abused and made the scorn of the nation? Those that were sound in the faith, how proper it was for them to labour for liberty, for a just liberty, that men should not be trampled on for their consciences! Had not they laboured, but lately under the weight of persecutions?

The "howling wildernesses" to which men had gone rather than betray their religion was New England; and there is a tradition, based on Clarendon's History of the Rebellion, that Cromwell himself would have joined the migration to America if the House of Commons had refused, in November, 1641, to pass the Grand Remonstrance that criticized the Stuart government for its policies both in Church and State.

2

Negotiation Preferable to Coercion

"WHATSOEVER WE GET BY A TREATY WILL BE FIRM AND DURABLE" [1]

In 1647, Cromwell, as second in command of the Parliamentary army under General Sir Thomas Fairfax, exerted all his efforts to find a settlement that would satisfy King, Parliament, and army. In his speeches to the Army Council, he argued that conciliation was better than imposing a decision by force.

We are now endeavouring as the main [part] of our work to make a preparation of somewhat that may tend to a general settlement of the peace of the kingdom and of the rights of the subject that justice and righteousness may peaceably flow out upon us. That's the main of our business. . . .

The way that our business is in is this: for the redressing of all these things it is a treaty, a treaty with commissioners sent from the Parliament down hither to the end that an happy issue may be put to all these matters that so much concern the good of the kingdom, and therein our good, is so that they must be finished in the way of a treaty. The truth of it is, you are all very reasonably sensible, that if those things were not removed that we think may lose us the fruit of a treaty, and the fruit of all our labours, it's vain to go on with a treaty and it's dangerous to be deluded by a treaty. And therefore I am confident of it that lest this inconveniency should come to us, lest there should come a second [civil] war, lest we should be deluded by a long treaty, your zeal hath been

---

[1] Speeches in the Army Council in Reading, July 16, 1647.

stirred up to express in your paper [a petition by the army agents or "Agitators"] that there is a necessity of a speedy marching [of the army] towards London to accomplish all these things. Truly I think that possibly that may be that which we shall be necessitated to do. Possibly it may be so; but yet I think it will be our honour and our honesty to do what we can to accomplish this work in the way of a treaty. And if I were able to give you all those reasons that lie in the case I think it would satisfy any rational man here. For certainly that is the most desirable way, and the other a way of necessity, and not to be done but in way of necessity.

And truly, instead of all reasons, let this serve: that whatsoever we get by a treaty, whatsoever comes to be settled upon us in that way, it will be firm and durable, it will be conveyed over to posterity as that which will be the greatest honour to us that ever poor creatures had, that we may obtain such things as these are which we are now about. And it will have firmness in it. We shall avoid the great objection that will lie against us that we have got things of the Parliament by force, and we know what it is to have that stain lie upon us. Things, though never so good, obtained in that way, it will exceedingly weaken the things both to ourselves and to all posterity. . . .

I hope in God that if we obtain these things in this way we propose to you and [at] this convenient time that we shall think ourselves very happy that we have not gone any other way for the obtaining them. That which we seek to avoid [is] the having of a second war and the defeating of those that are so dear to us, whose interest ought to be above our lives to us. If we find anything tending that way to delay us or disappoint us of those honest things we are to insist upon, I hope it cannot nor shall be doubted that the General [Fairfax] nor any of us will be backward for the accomplishment of those things that we have proposed. . . .

Really, really, have you what you will have, that [which] you have by force I look upon as nothing. I do not know that force is to be used except we cannot get what is for the good of the kingdom without force. . . .

It is the general good of them and all the people of the kingdom that's the question—what's for their good, not what pleases them. I do not know that all these considerations are arguments to have satisfaction in these things that we have in proposition. Though you be in the right and I in the wrong, if we be divided I doubt we shall all be in the wrong. . . .

"NOT WEDDED AND GLUED TO FORMS OF GOVERNMENT"[2]

In the end, anarchy in London compelled the army to march there and restore order during August. Cromwell's son-in-law, Henry Ireton, drafted heads of proposals for a political settlement, and Cromwell tried to persuade King Charles, a prisoner in the army's hands, to accept them. In the autumn, the army withdrew from London to Putney, where meetings of the Army Council were held in which representatives of the rising republican movement (such as Colonel Thomas Rainborowe, or Rainsborough) and of the left-wing political movement known as the Levelers (such as John Wildman), also were present. Again Cromwell urged conciliation and assured the Council that he was not committed to any particular course of action.

We are all here with the same integrity to the public; and perhaps we have all of us done our parts not frighted with difficulties, one as well as another; and I hope have all our purposes henceforward, through the grace of God, to do so still. And therefore truly I think all the consideration is that amongst us we are almost all soldiers; all considerations [of not fearing difficulties] or words of that kind do wonderfully please us, all words of courage animate us to carry on our business, to do God's business, that which is the will of God. I say it again, I do not think that any man here wants courage to do that which becomes an honest man and an Englishman to do. But we speak as men that have the fear of God before our eyes and men that may not resolve to do that which we do in the power of a fleshly strength, but to lay this as the foundation of all our actions—to do that which is the will of God. . . .

Concerning engagements and breaking of them: I do not think

² Speeches in the Army Council, October 28, 1647.

that it was at all offered by anybody that though an engagement were never so unrighteous, it ought to be kept. No man offered a syllable or a tittle [to this effect]. For certainly it's an act of duty to break an unrighteous engagement; he that keeps it does a double sin in that he made an unrighteous engagement and that he goes about to keep it. . . .

Perhaps we are upon engagements that we cannot with honesty break; but let me tell you this: that he that speaks to you of engagement here is as free from engagements to the King as any man in the world; and I know that if it were otherwise, I believe my future actions would provoke some to declare it. But I thank God I stand upon the bottom of my own innocence in this particular; through the grace of God I fear not the face of any man; I do not. . . .

[A proposal was made that the Council should pray to God for counsel, so that different points of view might be compromised.]

I hope we know God better than to make appearances of religious meetings cover for designs as for insinuations amongst you . . . For that's in all our hearts to profess above anything that's worldly the public good of the people; and if that be in our hearts truly and nakedly, I am confident it is a principle that will stand. Perhaps God may unite us and carry us both one way. . . .

[Speaking of proposals put forward to the Army Council by the Levelers and Agitators, Cromwell added:]

In general they aim at peace and safety, and really I am persuaded in my conscience it is their aim [to act] as may be most for the good of the people, for really if that be not the supreme good to us under God our principles fail. Now if that be in your spirits and our spirits it remains only that God show us the way and lead us in the way, which I hope He will. And give me leave [to add] that there may be some prejudices upon some of your spirits and such men that do affect your way that we may have some jealousies and apprehensions that we are wedded and glued to forms of government; so that whatsoever we may pretend, it is in vain to speak to us or to hope for any agreement from us to you; and, I believe, some such apprehensions as to some part of the legislative power of the kingdom where it may rest besides in the Commons of the kingdom. You will find that we are far from being so particularly engaged to anything to the prejudice of this—far from the notorious engagements that the world takes notice of—that we should not concur with you that the foundations and supremacy is in the people, radically in them, and to be set down by them in their representations . . .

Let us be doing, but let us be united in our doing.

"THE FACE OF AUTHORITY" [3]

Cromwell denied, in effect, that he had made any secret promises to maintain either the monarchy or the House of Lords. His mind was open about the future political settlement, though he thought that some of the proposals made by the Levelers tended toward anarchy. He accepted others of their proposals, however, such as abolition of the Royal veto, or "negative vote."

To that which hath been moved concerning the negative vote or things which have been delivered in papers or otherwise may present a real pleasing—I do not say that they have all pleased—for I think that the King is King by contract, and I shall say, as Christ said, "Let him that is without sin cast the first stone"; and mind that word of bearing one with another; it was taught to us today. If we had carried it on in the Parliament and by our power without any things laid on [us of] that kind so that we could say we were without transgression, I should then say it were just to cut off transgressors; but considering that we are in our own actions failing in many particulars, I think here is much necessity of pardoning the transgressors.

For the actions that are to be done and those that must do them: I think it is their proper place to conform to the Parliament that first gave them their being; and I think it is considerable [to be considered of] whether they do contrive to suppress the power of that power [Parliament] or no. If they do continue to suppress

[3] Speech to the Army Council, November 1, 1647.

them, how they can take the determination of commanding men, conducting men, quartering men, keeping guards without any authority otherwise than from themselves I am ignorant of. And therefore I think there is much need in the army to conform to those things that are within their sphere.

For those things that have been done [i.e. proposed] in the army —as this of *The Case of the Army truly Stated* [a political manifesto drawn up by John Wildman on behalf of the Levelers]—there is much in it useful and to be condescended to, but I am not satisfied how far we should press. Either they are a Parliament or no Parliament. If they be no Parliament, they are nothing and we are nothing likewise [since we are a Parliamentary army]. If they be a Parliament, we are to offer it to it. If we could see a visible presence of the people, either by subscriptions or number [I should be satisfied]; for in the government of nations that which is to be looked after is the affections of the people, and that I find which satisfies my conscience in the present thing.

Consider the case of the Jews. They were first divided into families where they lived, and had heads of families [to govern them]; they were next under judges, and then they were under kings: When they came to desire a king, they had a king; first elective and secondly by succession. In all these kinds of government they were happy and contented. If you make the best of it, if you should change the government to the best of it, it is but a [small] thing. It is but, as Paul says, "dross and dung in comparison with Christ"; and why shall we so far contest for temporal things yet if we cannot have this freedom we shall venture life and livelihood for it; when every man shall come to this condition, I think the State shall come to desolation. Therefore the considering of what is fit for the kingdom does belong to the Parliament—well composed in their creation and election—how far I shall leave it to the Parliament to offer it. There may be care that [lest] the elections or forms of Parliament are very illegal . . . I shall desire that there may be a form for the election of parliaments. And another thing [to be provided against] is the perpetuity of Parliaments . . . and for [among] other things that are to the King's negative vote, as may cast you off wholly, it hath been the resolution of the Parliament and of the Army. If there be a possibility of the Parliament's offering those things to the King that may secure us, I think there is much may be said for the doing of it.

As for the present condition of the army, I shall speak somewhat of it. For the conduct of the army, I perceive there are several declarations from the army and disobligations to the General's order by calling rendezvous and otherwise. I must confess I have a commission from the General and I understand what I am to do by it. I shall conform to him according to the rules and discipline of war . . . and therefore I conceive it is not in the power of any particular men or any particular man in the army to call a rendezvous of a troop or regiment or [in the] least to disoblige the army from those commands of the General. This way is destructive to the army and to every particular man in the army. I have been informed by some of the King's party that if they give us rope enough, we will hang ourselves. [We shall hang ourselves] if we do not conform to the rules of war, and therefore I shall move that we shall centre upon [them]. If it have but the face of authority, if it be but a hare swimming over the Thames, he will take hold of it, rather than let it go.

"WE WAIT UPON THE LORD" [4]

After the second civil war broke out in 1648, Cromwell still hoped for an agreed settlement, but he had ceased to trust King Charles and argued that fear of extremists like the Levelers should not be used as an excuse for allowing the King, who had provoked the war, to return to power.

I fear lest our friends should burn their fingers, as some others did not long since, whose hearts have ached for it. How easy is it to find arguments for what we would have; how easy to take offence at things called Levellers, and run into an extremity on the other hand, meddling with an accursed thing. Peace is only good when we receive it out of our Father's hand; it's dangerous to snatch at it, most dangerous to go against the will of God to attain it. War is good when led to by our Father, most evil when it comes from the

[4] Letter to Colonel Hammond, November 6, 1648.

lusts that are in our members. We wait upon the Lord, who will
teach us and lead us, whether to doing or suffering.

> *In this letter, Cromwell goes on to plead the case for union
> and mutual toleration among all the godly people (see p. 43
> below), and it is clear that at this time, he himself was con-
> templating the need to punish the King as a "man of blood"
> who had revived the civil war.*

3

The Execution of the King

Oliver Cromwell had declared that he was not "wedded and glued" to forms of government. Studying the Bible had revealed to him that God had approved for his Chosen People many different kinds of rule, ranging from judges to kings and from Moses to David. In common with other critics of King Charles's government, Cromwell had at first put the blame for its deficiencies upon wicked counsellors. Subsequently, he accepted the view that the fault lay not so much with the institution of monarchy as with the character of the monarch. Right up to 1649, Cromwell was willing to uphold the institution and even seems to have considered replacing Charles I with one of his sons if Charles refused to agree to the limitations upon his powers that were demanded by Parliament. It often is said by general historians and even by some biographers that Cromwell regarded the death of the King as a cruel necessity and that after the execution took place, he never referred to the event again, the implication being that he felt guilty and ashamed of what had been done. This is not so. Cromwell regarded the execution of Charles I as an act of justice upon a "man of blood" who had been responsible for deliberately launching the second civil war after he had been placed in honorable captivity and his followers had laid down their swords. The following extracts from Cromwell's letters and speeches refer to this.

"IMPARTIAL JUSTICE" [1]

I find a very great sense in the officers of the regiments of the sufferings and the ruin of this poor kingdom, and in them a very

---

[1] Letter to General Fairfax, November 20, 1648.

great zeal to have impartial justice done upon offenders; and I must confess I do in all from my heart concur with them; and I verily think and am persuaded they are things which God puts into our hearts.

"EXEMPLARY JUSTICE" [2]

You know how it hath pleased God to beat down all your enemies under your feet, both in this kingdom and the kingdom of Scotland; and you have with simplicity of heart made this opposition to those enemies upon those honest and religious grounds that it is fit for godly and honest and religious men to propose to themselves; and God hath brought the war to an issue here, and given you a great fruit of that war, to wit: the execution of exemplary justice upon the prime leader of all this quarrel into the three kingdoms and of divers persons of very great quality, who did cooperate with him in the destruction of this kingdom.

CASTING OFF TYRANNY [3]

Arbitrary powers men begin to weary of, in Kings and Churchmen; their juggle between them mutually to uphold civil and ecclesiastical tyranny begins to be transparent. Some have cast off both; and hope by the grace of God to keep it so.

IN ANSWER TO THEIR CONSCIENCES [4]

If the civil authority or that part of it which continued to be faithful to their trust [i.e., Parliament after it had been "purged" by the army in 1648] true to the ends of the Covenant, did, in answer to their consciences, turn out a tyrant, in a way which Christians in aftertimes will mention with honour, and all tyrants in the world look at with fear, and if while many thousands of saints in England rejoice to think of it, and have received from the hand of God a liberty from the fear of like usurpations, and have cast off

[2] Speech to General Council of Officers, March 23, 1649.
[3] Declaration to the Irish, January, 1650.
[4] Letter to the Governor of Edinburgh Castle, September 12, 1650.

him [Charles II] who trod in his father's footsteps, doing mischief as far as he was able (who you [the Scots] have received like fire in your bosom—of which God will, I trust, in time make you sensible): if ministers railing at the civil power, and calling them murderers and the like for doing these things, have been dealt with as you mention—will this be found a personal persecution? Or is sin so because they say so? They that have acted this great business [judging and executing Charles I] have given reason of their faith in the action; and some here are ready further to do it against all gainsayers.

But it will be found that these reproved do not only make themselves the judges and determiners of sin that so they may reprove, but they also took the liberty to stir up the people to blood and arms; and would have brought a war upon England, as hath been upon Scotland, had not God prevented it. And if such severity as hath been expressed towards them be worthy of the name of personal persecution, let all uninterested men judge. . . .

4

The Frame of Government

Granted that a revolution had taken place and that a "tyranny" had been destroyed, what form of government did Cromwell wish to see set up? Some authors have described him as a conservative mainly concerned with maintaining and promoting the interests of his own class, being anxious in particular to preserve the institution of private property. Others have thought of him as a kind of anarchist, and, at least by the Royalists of his own day, he was regarded as a subversive character. In the following quotations, his anxiety to procure a firm and lasting political settlement and to prevent anarchy from breaking out and his spirit of compromise will be illustrated. And his exposition of what he held to be the case for having a stable government and a balanced constitution when, as a result of the promulgation of what was known as the Instrument of Government, he himself had been appointed chief executive under the name of Lord Protector, will be set forth.

"WE DESIRE A SETTLEMENT" [1]

For the thing we insist upon as Englishmen—and surely our being soldiers hath not stript us of that interest, although our malicious enemies would have it so, we desire a settlement of the peace of the kingdom and of the liberties of the subject, according to the votes and declarations of Parliament, which, before we took up arms, were, by the Parliament, used as arguments and inducements to invite us and divers of our dear friends out; some of which have lost their lives in this war, which being, by God's blessing, finished, we think we have as much right to demand, and desire to

[1] A letter addressed to the Lord Mayor, Aldermen and Common Council of the City of London and signed, among others, by Cromwell.

see, a happy settlement, as we have to our money and the other common interest of soldiers which we have insisted upon. We find also the ingenious and honest people, in almost all parts of the kingdom where we come, full of the sense of ruin and misery if the army should be disbanded before the peace of the kingdom, and those other things before mentioned, have a full and perfect settlement.

We have said before, and profess it now, we desire no alteration of the civil government. We desire not to intermeddle with, or at least to interrupt, the settling of the Presbyterial Government. Nor do we seek to open a way to licentious liberty, under pretence of obtaining ease for tender consciences.

We profess, as ever in these things, when the State have once made a settlement, we have nothing to say but to submit or suffer. Only we could wish that every good citizen, and every man that walks peaceably in a blameless conversation, and is beneficial to the Commonwealth, may have liberty and encouragement; it being according to the just policy of States, even to justice itself.

DANGERS OF ANARCHY [2]

Truly this paper [the "Agreement of the People" put forward by the political group known as the Levelers] does contain in it very great alterations of the very government of the kingdom, alterations from that government that it hath been under, I believe I may almost say, since it hath been a nation. . . . How do we know if, whilst we are disputing these things, another company of men shall gather together and they shall put out a paper as plausible perhaps as this? I do not know why it might not be done by that time you have agreed upon this or got hands to it, if that be the way. And not only another and another, but many of this kind. And if so, what do you think the consequences would be? Would it not be confusion? Would it not be utter confusion? Would it not make England like the Switzerland country, one canton of the Swiss against another, and one county against another? I ask you whether it be not fit for every honest man seriously to lay that upon his heart? And if so, what would that produce but an absolute

[2] Speech to Army Council, October 28, 1647.

desolation—an absolute desolation to the nation—and we in the meantime tell the nation: "It is for your liberty, 'tis for your privilege, 'tis for your good." Pray God it prove so whatever course we run. . . . I know a man may answer all difficulties with faith, and faith will answer all difficulties really where it is, and we are very apt, all of us, to call that faith that perhaps may be but carnal imagination and carnal reasonings. . . .

THE FOUR FUNDAMENTALS [3]

Some things are fundamentals about which I shall deal plainly with you: They may not be parted with; but will, I trust, be delivered over to posterity, as being the fruits of our blood and travail. The Government by a Single Person and a Parliament is fundamental! It is the *esse,* it is constitutive. And for the person—though I may seem to plead for myself, yet I do not: no, nor can any reasonable man say it. But if the things throughout this speech be true, I plead for this nation, and all honest men therein who have borne their testimony as aforesaid, and not for myself. And if things should do otherwise than well—which I would not fear—and the common enemy and discontented persons take advantage of these distractions, the issue will be put before God: let Him own it or let Him disown it as He please!

In every government there must be somewhat fundamental, somewhat like a Magna Carta that should be standing and unalterable. . . . That parliaments should not make themselves perpetual is a fundamental. Of what assurance is a law to prevent so great an evil if it lie in one or the same legislature to unlaw it again? Is this like to be lasting? It will be like a rope of sand; and it will give no security; for the same men may unbuild what they have built.

Is not liberty of conscience in religion a fundamental? So long as there is liberty of conscience for the supreme magistrate to exercise his conscience in erecting what form of church government he is satisfied he should set up, why should he not give it to others [that is, he must grant full liberty to dissent]. Liberty of conscience is a natural right; and he that would have it ought to give it; having liberty to settle what he likes for the public. Indeed that hath been

[3] Speech to the first Protectorate parliament, September 12, 1654.

one of the vanities of our contests. Every sect saith: "Oh, give me liberty!" but give him it, and to his power he will not yield it to anybody else. Where is our ingenuousness? Truly, that's a thing that ought to be very reciprocal! The magistrate hath his supremacy, and he may settle religion [that is, the government of the Church] according to his conscience. And I may say it to you, I can say it: all the money of this nation would not have tempted men to fight upon such an account as they have engaged in, if they had not had hopes of liberty better than they had from episcopacy or than would have been afforded them from a Scottish presbytery—or an English either, if it had made such steps or had been as sharp and rigid as it threatened when it was first set up. This, I say, is a fundamental. It ought to be so. It is for us and the generations to come. And if there be an absoluteness in the imposer, without fitting allowances and exceptions from the rule, we shall have our people driven into wildernesses, as they were, when those poor and afflicted people, that forsook their estates and inheritances here, where they lived plentifully and comfortably, for the enjoyment of their liberty were necessitated to go into a vast howling wilderness in New England—where they have, for liberty's sake, stripped themselves of all their comfort and the full enjoyment they had, embracing rather loss of friends and want than be so ensnared and in bondage.

Another [fundamental] which I had forgotten is the militia [that is, control of the armed forces]. That is judged a fundamental if anything be so. That it should be well and equally placed is very necessary. For, put the absolute power of the militia into one [hand] without check, what doth it? I pray you, what check is there upon your perpetual parliaments, if the government be wholly stripped of this, of the militia? It is equally placed and desires were to have it so—namely in one person and the parliament, while parliament sits. What signifies a provision against perpetuating of parliaments if this be solely in them? Whether without check the parliament have not liberty to alter the frame of government—to aristocracy, to democracy, to anarchy, to anything, if this be fully in them? Yea, into all confusion; and that without remedy! And if this one thing be placed in one [hand], that one be it parliament, be it supreme governor, they or he hath power to make what they please of all the rest. Therefore if you would have a balance at all and [if you agree] that some fundamentals must stand which may be worthy to be delivered over to posterity, truly I think it is not unreasonably urged that the militia should be disposed as it is laid down in the [Instrument of] Government: and that it should equally be that neither one person in parliament nor out of parliament should have the power of ordering it. The Council [of State] are trustees of the Commonwealth in all the intervals of parliaments; who have as absolute a negative upon the supreme officer in the said intervals as the parliament while it is sitting. It [the army] cannot be made use of; not a man can be raised nor a penny charged upon the people; nothing done without consent of parliament; and in all the intervals of parliament without consent of the Council, it is not to be exercised . . .

5
Liberty of Conscience

*Oliver Cromwell fought in the civil war above
all because he wished to insure liberty of conscience for all
Christians and their freedom from the "tyranny" of the
Bishops. He was equally opposed to Scottish presbyterianism
and Anglican episcopalianism as well as to Roman Catholicism or what he called "popery." As Lord Protector, from
1653 until his death, he consistently upheld liberty of conscience, though he favored a general framework of Church
government and continued payment of the clergy out of
tithes until some better way of paying them should be found.
Even before he became Protector, he pleaded with Parliament
for liberty of conscience.*

AFTER NASEBY [1]

Honest men served you faithfully in this action [the victory
of Naseby]. Sir, they are trusty; I beseech you in the name of God
not to discourage them. I wish this action may beget thankfulness
and humility in all that are concerned in it. He that ventures his
life for the liberty of his country, I wish he trust God for the liberty
of his conscience, and you for the liberty he fights for.

AFTER BRISTOL [2]

Sir, they that have been employed in this service know that
faith and prayer obtained this city for you: I do not say ours only
but of the people of God with you and all England over, who
have wrestled with God for a blessing in this very thing. Our desires are that God may be glorified by the same spirit of faith by

---

[1] Letter to the Speaker of the House of Commons, June 15, 1645.
[2] Letter to the Speaker, September 14, 1645.

which we asked all our sufficiency, and having received it, it's meet that He have all the praise. Presbyterians, Independents, all had here the same spirit of faith and prayer: the same pretence and answer; they agree here, know no names of difference: pity it is that it should be otherwise anywhere. All that believe have the real unity, which is most glorious because inward and spiritual, in the Body and to the Head. As for being united in forms, commonly called uniformity, every Christian will for peace-sake study and do as far as conscience will permit; and from brethren in things of the mind we look for no compulsion but that of light and reason.

AFTER DUNBAR [3]

Indeed you err through mistaking of the Scriptures. Approbation [that is, ordination of preachers by the Church] is an act of conveniency in respect of order; not of necessity to give faculty to preach the Gospel. Your pretended fear lest error should step in is like the man who would keep all wine out [of] the country lest men should be drunk. It will be found an unjust and unwise jealousy to deny a man the liberty he has by nature upon the supposition he may abuse it. When he doth abuse it, judge. If a man speak foolishly, ye suffer him gladly because ye are wise; if erroneously, the truth more appears by your conviction. Stop such a man's mouth with sound word that cannot be gainsaid. If [he speak] blasphemously or to the disturbance of the public peace, let the civil magistrate punish him; if truly, rejoice in the truth.

"I HAVE BORNE MY REPROACH" [4]

I will tell you the truth: Our practice since the last parliament hath been to let all this nation see that whatever pretensions to religion would keep quiet, peaceable, they should enjoy conscience and liberty to themselves; and not make religion a pretence for arms and blood, truly we have suffered them, and that cheerfully, to enjoy their own liberties. Whatsoever is contrary, let the pretence be never so specious—if it tend to combination, to inter-

[3] Letter to the Governor of Edinburgh, September 12, 1650.
[4] Speech to second Protectorate parliament, September 17, 1656.

ests and factions, we shall not care by the grace of God whom we shall meet withall, I am against all liberty of conscience repugnant to this. I am. If men will profess, be they those under Baptism [Baptists], be they those of the Independent judgment simply, and of the Presbyterian judgment, in the name of God encourage them, countenance them; so long as they do plainly continue to be thankful to God, and make use of the liberty given them to enjoy their own consciences! For, as it was said today, undoubtedly this is the peculiar interest all this while contested for.

That men that believe in Jesus Christ—that's the form that gives the being to true religion, faith in Christ and walking in a profession answerable to that faith; men that believe the remission of sins through the blood of Christ and live upon the grace of God: that those men that are certain they are so are members of Jesus Christ and are to Him as the apple of IIis eye. Whoever hath this faith, let his form be what it will; he walking peaceably, without the prejudicing of others under another form—it is a debt due to God and Christ; and He will require it if he may not enjoy liberty.

If a man of one form will be trampling upon the heels of another form; if an Independent, for example, will despise him under Baptism and will revile him and reproach and provoke him, I will not suffer it in him. If, on the other side, those of the Anabaptists shall be censuring the godly ministers of the nation that profess under that of Independency; or those that profess under Presbytery shall be reproaching or speaking evil of them, traducing and censuring them—as I would not be willing to see the day on which England shall be in the power of Presbytery to impose upon the consciences of others that profess faith in Christ—so I will not endure to reproach them. But God give us hearts and spirits to keep things equal. Which, truly, I must profess to you, hath been my temper. I have had boxes [buffets] and rebukes, on the one hand and on the other; some censuring me for Presbytery; others [as] an inletter of all the sects and heresies in the nation. I have borne my reproach: but I have through God's mercy not been unhappy in preventing any one religion impose upon another.

6
Cromwell as Reformer

It sometimes is said that once the monarchy had been overthrown, Cromwell lacked progressive and constructive ideas and was content to impose a conservative dictatorship. But there is adequate, if scattered, evidence that he was anxious to reform the laws and even revolutionize the structure of society.

"RELIEVE THE OPPRESSED" [1]

It is easy to say the Lord hath done this [won the battle of Dunbar over a larger number of Scots]. It would do you good to see and hear our poor foot go up and down making their boast of God. But, Sir, it is in your hands, and by these eminent mercies God puts its more into your hands, to give glory to Him: to improve your power and His blessings, to His praise. We that serve you beg of you not to own us, but God alone; we pray you own His people more and more, for they are the chariots and horsemen of Israel. Disown yourselves, but own your authority, and improve it to curb the proud and insolent, such as would disturb the tranquillity of England, though under what specious pretences soever; relieve the oppressed, hear the groans of poor prisoners in England; be pleased to reform the abuses of all professions; and if there be any one that makes many poor to make a few rich, that suits not a Commonwealth. If He that strengthens your servants to fight, pleases to give you the hearts to set upon these things, in order to His glory and the glory of your Commonwealth, besides the benefit England shall feel thereby, you shall shine forth to other nations, who shall emulate the glory of such a pattern, and through the power of God turn it into the like.

[1] Letter to the Speaker, September 4, 1650.

"JUST MEN AND PLAIN LAWS" [2]

It [the Protectorate Government] hath had some things in desire; and it hath done some things actually. It hath desire to reform the laws—to reform them: and for that end it hath called together persons—without offence be it spoken—of as great ability and as great integrity as are in these nations, to consider how the laws might be made less onerous to the people; how to lessen expense, for the good of the nation. And those things are in preparation and Bills prepared; which, in due time, I make no question, will be tendered to you.

There hath been care taken to put the administration of the laws into the hand of just men: men of the most known integrity and ability. The Chancery hath been reformed; and, I hope, to the just satisfaction of good men; and to the things depending there which made the burden and work of the honourable persons intrusted in those services too heavy for their ability, it hath referred many of them to those places where Englishmen love to have their rights tried—the Courts of Law at Westminster.

"WICKED LAWS A GREAT GRIEF" [3]

There is one general grievance in the nation: it is the law. Not that laws are grievance; but there are laws that are a grievance; and the great grievance lies in the execution and administration. I think I may say it: I have as eminent judges in this land as have been had, or that the nation has had for these many years. Truly, I could be particular as to the executive part, to the administration; but that would trouble you. But the truth of it is—there are wicked, abominable laws that it will be in your power to alter. To hang a man for a trifle and pardon murder—it is the ministration of the law through the ill-framing of it. I have known in my experience abominable murders [ac]quitted. And to come and see men lose their lives for petty matters: this is a thing God will reckon for. And I wish it may not lie upon this nation a day

[2] Speech to Parliament, September 4, 1654.
[3] Speech to Parliament, September 17, 1656.

longer than you have the opportunity to give a remedy; and I hope I shall cheerfully join with you in it. This hath been a great grievance to many honest hearts and conscientious people; and I hope it is in all your hearts to rectify it.

PROMOTING LEARNING A MATTER OF GREAT CONCERN [4]

Having received information from the Mayor and citizens of Durham and some gentlemen of the northern counties that upon their petition to the Parliament that the houses of the late Dean and Chapter of the city of Durham might be converted into a college or school of literature the Parliament was pleased in May last to refer the same to the committee for removing obstructions in the sale of Dean-and-Chapter lands to consider thereof and to report their opinion to the House: which said committee (as I am also informed) have so far approved thereof as that they are of the opinion that the said houses will be a fit place to erect a college or school for all the sciences and literature and that it will be a pious and laudable work and of great use to the northern parts. . . .

Truly it seems to me a matter of great concernment and importance as that which, by the blessing of God, may much conduce to the promoting of learning and piety in those poor rude and ignorant parts; there being also many concurring advantages to this place as to pleasantness and aptness of situation and plenty of provisions, which seem to favour and plead for their desires therein. And besides the good (so obvious to us) those northern counties may reap thereby, who knows but the setting on foot of this work at this time may suit with God's present dispensations; and may (if due care and circumspection be used in the right constituting and carrying on the same) tend to, and (by the blessing of God) produce such happy and glorious fruits as are scarce thought on or foreseen!

"REFORMATION OF MANNERS" [5]

I did hint to you my thoughts about the reformation of manners; and those abuses that are in this nation through disorder is

[4] Letter to the Speaker of the Parliament of the Commonwealth of England from Edinburgh, March 11, 1650.
[5] Speech of September 17, 1656.

a thing which should be much in your hearts. It is that that I am confident is a description and character of that interest you have been engaged against, and pressing to as any other against the badge and character of countenancing profaneness, disorder and wickedness in all places, and whatsover is next of kin to that, and most agrees with that, which is popery and the profane nobility and gentry of this nation. In my conscience, it was a shame to be a Christian within these fifteen, sixteen, or seventeen years in this nation either or elsewhere. It was a shame, it was a reproach to a man; and the badge of Puritan was put upon it. We would keep up the nobility and gentry—and the way to keep them up is not to suffer them to be patronisers nor countenancers of debauchery or disorders. And you will hereby be as labourers in the work. And a man may tell as plainly as can be what becomes of us if we grow indifferent and lukewarm under I know not what weak pretensions. If it lives in us therefore; I say if it be in the general, it is a thing I am confident our liberty and prosperity depends upon—reformation. To make it a shame to see men to be bold in sin and profaneness—and God will bless you. You will be a blessing to the nation; and by this be more the repairers of breaches than anything in the world. Truly these things do respect the souls of men, and the spirits—which *are* the men. The mind is the man. If that be kept pure, a man signifies somewhat; if not, I would very fain see what difference there is betwixt him and a beast. He hath only some activity to do some more mischief.

7
Cromwell the Patriot

Cromwell was unashamedly a patriot, first and foremost an Englishman. He was doubtful about the wisdom of calling in the Scots, as John Pym had done in 1643, to help the Parliamentarians defeat the Royalists in the civil wars. Later, he was obliged to fight against the Scots twice, in 1648 and in 1650–51, and also to campaign against the Irish. He believed that all three nations could be successfully united into one British Commonwealth, but only if they were prepared to accept leadership from London.

THE BRITISH [1]

When I first met you [representatives of England, Scotland and Ireland in the first Protectorate Parliament] in this room, it was my apprehension the hopefullest day that ever mine eyes saw as to considerations of this world. For I did look at, as wrapt up in you together with myself, the hopes and the happiness of— though not the greatest—yet a very great and the best people in the world. And truly and unfeignedly I thought so: as a people that have the highest and clearest profession among them of the greatest glory, to wit, religion: as a people that have been, like other nations, sometimes up and sometimes down in our honour in the world, but yet never so low but we might measure with other nations: and a people that have had a stamp upon them from God; God having, as it were, summed up all our former honour and glory in the things that are of glory to nations, in an epitome, within these last ten or twelve years last past!

[1] Speech of January 22, 1655.

THE ENGLISH [2]

We are apt to boast sometimes we are Englishmen: and truly it is no shame to us that we are so; but it is a motive to us to do like Englishmen and seek the real good of this nation and the interest of it.

THE SCOTS [3]

I profess to thee I desire from my heart, I have prayed for it, I have waited for the day to see union and right understanding between the godly people (Scots, English, Jews, Gentiles, Presbyterians, Independents, Anabaptists, and all). Our brothers of Scotland (really Presbyterians) were our greatest enemies. God hath justified us in their sight, caused us to requite good for evil, caused them to acknowledge it publicly by acts of state, and privately, and the thing is true in the sight of the sun. It is a high conviction upon them. Was it not fit to be civil, to profess love, to deal with clearness with them for removing of prejudice, to ask them what they had against us, and to give them an honest answer? This we have done, and not more. And herein is a more glorious work in our eyes than if we had gotten the sacking and plunder of Edinburgh, the strong castles in our hands, and made conquest from Tweed to the Orcades; and we can say, through God we have left by the grace of God such a witness amongst them as if it work not, yet there is that conviction upon them that will undoubtedly bear its fruit in due time.

(1650) [4]

Since we came in Scotland, it hath been our desire and longing to have avoided blood in this business by reason that God hath a people here fearing His name, though deceived.

[2] Speech of January 25, 1658.
[3] Letter to Colonel Robert Hammond, November 6, 1648.
[4] Letter to the Speaker, September 4, 1650.

(1658) [5]

And hath Scotland been long settled? Have not they a like sense of poverty [with the Irish]? I speak plainly. In good earnest I do not think the Scots nation have been under as great a suffering in point of livelihood and subsistence outwardly as any people I have named to you. I do truly think they are a very ruined nation. Yet in a way (I have spoken to some gentlemen come from thence) hopeful enough yet—it hath pleased God to give that plentiful encouragement to the meaner sort in Scotland. The meaner sort live as well and are likely to come into as thriving a condition under your government as when they were under their great lords, who made them work for their living no better than the peasants of France. I am loath to speak anything that may reflect upon that nation; but the middle sort of this people grow up into such substance as makes their lives comfortable, if not better than they were before.

THE IRISH [6]

Cromwell's attitude toward the Irish was influenced by their rebellion against the English in 1641 and by the support given by the Irish Royalists and Roman Catholics to the Stuart cause both before and after the execution of Charles I. The following passage has been rightly described as a ludicrous view of Irish history. It is taken from the declaration Cromwell made as Lord Lieutenant and commander-in-chief after he was appointed to those posts by the English Parliament in 1649.

By the grace of God, we fear not, we care not for your union. Your covenant is with Death and Hell! Your union is like that of Simeon and Levi: associate yourselves, and you shall be broken in pieces; take counsel together, and it shall come to naught. For though it becomes us to be humble in respect of ourselves, yet we can say to you: God is not with you. You say your union is against

[5] Speech of January 25, 1658.
[6] Declaration of January, 1650.

a common enemy: and to this, if you will be talking of union, I will give you some wormwood to bite on; by which it will appear God is not with you.

Who is it that created this common enemy? I suppose you mean Englishmen. The English. Remember, ye hypocrites, Ireland was once united to England. Englishmen had good inheritances which many of them purchased with their money; they or their ancestors from many of you and your ancestors. They lived peaceably and honestly amongst you. You had generally equal benefit of the protection of England with them and equal justice from the laws— saving what was necessary for the State (out of reasons of State) to put some few people apt to rebel on the instigation of such as you. You broke this union! You, unprovoked, put the English to the most unheard-of and most unprovoked massacre (without respect of sex or age) that ever the sun beheld. And at a time when Ireland was in perfect peace and when, through the example of English industry, through commerce and traffic, that which was in the natives' hands was better to them than if all Ireland had been in their possession, and not an Englishman in it.

8
Cromwell's Foreign Policy

Cromwell's foreign policy was guided by three main considerations: (1) the interest of the Commonwealth, which included securing freedom of the seas to British ships and promoting international trade; (2) support for the Protestant interest in Europe; (3) resistance to Spain, a kingdom he regarded as the traditional enemy of Great Britain, both at home and abroad, since the time when Philip II attempted to overthrow Queen Elizabeth. To pursue these aims, Cromwell, when Lord Protector, concluded treaties of peace and commerce with the Protestant European countries, including the United Netherlands, with which the English republic had been at war from 1652 to 1654; he waged against Spain "beyond the line," in the West Indies, a war that developed into a European war by 1656; and he came to terms with France because France was at war with Spain and with Portugal, the latter being also the enemy of Spain. He outlined his conduct of foreign affairs in three speeches to Parliament.

PEACE WITH HONOR [1]

[After the death of Charles I and the consequent wars in Ireland and Scotland in 1649–51] to add yet to our misery whilst we were in this condition, we were in war, deeply engaged in a war with Portugal [which had lent support to the Royalists] whereby our trade ceased and the evil consequences by that war were manifest and very considerable. And not only this, but we had a war with Holland; consuming our treasure, occasioning a vast burden upon the people; a war that cost this nation full as much as the

[1] Speech to the first Protectorate Parliament, September 4, 1654.

46

taxes came unto; the navy being a hundred and sixty ships, which cost this nation above £100,000 a month; besides the contingencies, which would make it £120,000 a month. That very one war did engage us to so great a charge. At the same time we were also at war with France. The advantages that were taken at the discontents and divisions among ourselves did also foment that war, and at least hinder us of an honourable peace: every man being confident we could not hold out long. And surely they did not calculate amiss, if the Lord had not been exceeding gracious to us! . . . And besides the sufferings in respect to the trade of the nation, it's most evident that the purse of the nation had not possibly been able longer to bear it—by reasons of the advantages taken by other States to improve their own and spoil our manufacture of cloth and hinder the event thereof; which is the great staple commodity of this nation. This was our condition: spoiled in our trade, and we at this vast expense; thus dissettled at home and having these engagements abroad.

. . . The wars did exhaust our treasure and put you into such a condition that you must have sunk therein, if it had continued but for a few months longer: this I can affirm if strong probability be a fit ground. You have now [1654] (though it be not the first in time) peace with Swedeland; . . . an honourable peace with a kingdom that, not many years since, was such a friend to France, and lately perhaps inclinable enough to the Spaniard. And I believe you expect not very much good from any of your Catholic neighbours; nor yet that they would be very willing you should have a good understanding with your Protestant friends. Yet, thanks be to God, that peace is concluded. . . .

You have a peace with the Dane, a State that lay contiguous to the part of this island which hath given us the most trouble [Scotland]. And certainly if your enemies abroad be able to annoy you, it is likely they will take their advantage (where it best lies) to give you trouble there. But you have a peace there and an honourable one. Satisfaction for your merchants' ships; not only to their content but to their rejoicing. . . . You have the [Baltic] Sound open; which was obstructed. That which was and is the strength of this nation, the shipping, will not be supplied thence. And whereas you were glad to have anything of that kind [naval supplies] at the second hand, you have now all manner of commerce, and at as much freedom as the Dutch themselves there at the same rate and toll; and I think you may say by that peace [treaty] the said rates now fixed cannot be raised to you.

You have a peace with the Dutch: a peace unto which I shall say little because so well known is the benefit and consequences of it. And I think it was as desirable and acceptable to the spirit of this nation as any one thing that lay before us. And as I believe nothing so much gratified our enemies as to see us at odds, so I persuade myself that nothing is of more terror or trouble to them than to see us reconciled. As a peace with Protestant states hath much security in it, so it hath much of honor and of assurance to the Protestant interest abroad; without which no assstance can be given thereunto. I wish it may be written upon our hearts to be zealous for that interest! For if ever it were like to come under a condition of suffering, it is now. In all the Emperor's patrimonial territories, the endeavour is to drive them [the Protestants] out as fast as they can; and they are necessitated to run to Protestant States to seek their bread. And by this conjunction of interests [the Anglo-Dutch alliance] I hope you will be in a more fit capacity to help them. And it begets some reviving of their spirits that you will help them as opportunity shall serve.

You have a peace likewise with the Crown of Portugal; which peace, though it hung long in hand, yet is lately concluded. It is a peace that, your merchants make us believe, is of good concernment to their trade; their assurance [security] being greater, and so their profit in trade thither than to other places. And this hath been obtained in that treaty, which never was since the Inquisition was set up there: that our people which trade thither have liberty of consciences. . . .

Indeed peace is, as you were well told today, desirable with all men, as far as it may be had with conscience and honour! We are upon a treaty with France. And we may say this, that if God give us honour in the eyes of the nations about us, we have reason to bless Him for it, and so to own it. And I dare say that there is not a nation in Europe but they are very willing to ask a good understanding with you.

"YOUR GREAT ENEMY IS THE SPANIARD" [2]

Why, truly, your great enemy is the Spaniard. He is. He is a natural enemy. He is naturally so; he is naturally so throughout, by reason of that enmity that is in him against whatsoever is of God. . . . With this King and State, I say, you are at this present in hostility. We put you into this hostility. You will give us leave to tell you how. As we are ready to excuse most of our actions—aye, and to justify them as well as to excuse them—upon the grounds of necessity; the grounds of necessity being above all considerations of justification, of instituted law; and if this or any other State should go about—as I know they never will—to make laws against what *may* happen, I think it is obvious to any man they will be making laws against Providence; events, and issues of things being from God alone, to whom all issues belong.

The Spaniard is your enemy; and is your enemy (as I told you) naturally, by that antipathy that is in him providentially, and that in diverse respects. You could not have an honest or honourable peace with him: it was sought by the Long Parliament; it was not attained. It could not be attained with honour and honesty. And truly when I say that, he is naturally throughout an enemy; an enmity is put into him by God. "I will put an enmity between thy seed and her seed"—which goes for little among statesmen but is more considerable than all things! . . .

No sooner did this nation reform that which is called (unworthily) the Reformed Religion after the death of Queen Mary, by Queen Elizabeth of famous memory,—we need not be ashamed to call her so—but the Spaniard's design became, by all unworthy, unnatural means, to destroy that person, and to seek the ruin and destruction of these kingdoms. And for me to instance in particulars upon that account were to trouble you at a very unseasonable time. . . . But his enmity was upon that general account which all are agreed. The French, all the Protestants in Germany have agreed that his design was the empire of the whole Christian world, if not more—and upon that ground he looks at this nation as his greatest obstacle. And what his attempts were in that end I refer you to

[2] Speech to Parliament, September 17, 1656.

that declaration [by the Council of State in October, 1655] and to the observations of men who read history. It would not be difficult to call to mind the several assassinations designed upon that lady, the great Queen [Elizabeth]: the attempts upon Ireland, the Spaniards invading of it; the designs of the same nature upon this nation—public designs, private designs, all manner of designs to accomplish this great and general end. Truly King James [I] made a peace; but whether this nation and the interests of all Protestant Christians suffered not more by that peace than ever by Spain's hostility I refer to your consideration.

So that a State that you can neither have peace with nor reason from is that State with whom you have enmity at this time and against whom you are engaged. And give me leave to say this unto you, because it is the truth, and most men know it, that the Long Parliament did endeavour, but could not obtain satisfaction all the time they sat; for their messenger [the ambassador to Spain, Anthony Ascham] was murdered; and when they asked satisfaction for the blood of your poor people that traded thither, satisfaction in none of these things would be given, but was denied. I say they denied satisfaction to be given either for your messenger that was murdered or the blood that was shed or the damages that were done in the West Indies. No satisfaction at all; nor any reason given why there should not be liberty given to your people that traded thither, whose trade was very considerable there and drew many of your people thither; and begot an apprehension in us. . . . But all of us know that the people that went thither to manage the trade there were imprisoned there. We desired such liberty as that they might keep their Bibles in their pockets, to exercise their liberty of religion to themselves, and not to be under restraint. But there is not liberty of conscience to be had; neither satisfaction for injuries nor for blood; but when these things were desired, the ambassador told us: "It was to ask his master's two eyes"; to ask both his eyes, to ask these things of him!

Now if this be so, why truly then there is some little foundation laid to justify the war that has been entered upon with the Spaniard. And not only so: but the plain truth of it: make peace with any State that is Popish and subjected to the determination of Rome and the Pope himself—you are bound and they are loose. It is in the pleasure of the Pope at any time to tell you that though a man be murdered, yet his murderer has got into sanctuary! And it is as true, and it hath been found by common and constant experience, that peace is but to be kept so long as the Pope saith Amen to it. We have not to do with any Popish State except France: and it is certain they do not think themselves under such a tie to the Pope; but think themselves at liberty to perform honesty with nations with whom they are agreed, and protest against the obligation of such a thing as that is. They are able to give us an explicit answer to anything reasonably demanded of them: and there is no State we can speak of save this but will break their promise or keep it as they pleased upon these grounds—being under the lash of the Pope, to be by him determined.

In the time when Philip the Second was married to Queen Mary, and since that time, through that Power and [its] instigation twenty thousand Protestants were massacred in Ireland. We thought, being denied just things—we thought it our duty to get that by the sword which was not to be had otherwise. And this hath been the spirit of Englishmen; and if so, certain it is, and ought to be, the spirits of men that have higher spirits. With this State you are engaged. And it is a great and powerful State—though I may say that also with all other States, with all other Christian States, you are at peace, and all these other engagements were upon you before this Government was undertaken: which was war with France, Denmark and, upon that matter, with Spain. I could instance how it was said: "We will have a war in the Indies, though we fight them not at home." I say: we are at peace with all other nations and have only a war with Spain.

"FIGHT TO DEFEND YOURSELVES" [3]

What are the affairs, I beseech you, abroad? I thought the profession of the Protestant religion was a thing of well-being; and truly, in a good sense, it is so, and it's no more: though it be a very high thing, it's but a thing of well-being. But take it with all the complications of it, with all the circumstances of it, with respect had to the nations abroad, and I do believe that he that looks

[3] Speech to Parliament, January 25, 1658.

well about him and considereth the state of the Protestant affairs all
Christendom over, he must needs say and acknowledge that the
greatest design now on foot, in comparison of which all other designs are but little things, is whether the Christian world shall be
all Popery or whether God hath a love to, and we ought to have a
brotherly fellow-feeling of the interest of all the Protestant Christians in the world? And he that strikes at but one species of a general to make it nothing, strikes at all.

Is it not so now that the Protestant cause and interest abroad is
struck at; and is, in opinion and apprehension, quite under foot
trodden down? And judge with me a little, I beseech you, whether
it be so or no. And then, I pray you, will you consider how far we
are concerned in that danger as to being!

We have known very well that that which is accounted the honest
and religious interest of this nation, it was not trodden under foot
all at once but by degrees—that that interest might be consumed
as with a canker insensibly, as Jonah's gourd was till it was quite
withered in a night. It is at another rate now! For certainly this, in
the general: the Papacy and those that are upholders of it, they
have openly avowedly trodden God's people under foot, on that
very notion and account that they were Protestant. The money
you parted with in that noble charity that was exercised with in
this nation, and the just sense that you had of those poor Pied-
montese [for whom the money was collected] was satisfaction
enough to yourselves of that. As a precursory thing if all the Protestants in Europe had had but that head, that head had been cut
off, and so to an end of all. Is that all? No. Look but how the
House of Austria [that is, the Habsburgs] on both sides of Christendom are armed and prepared to make themselves able to destroy
the whole Protestant interest. . . .

But it may be said: "This is a great way off, in the extremist
parts of it [Europe]; what is that to us?" If it be nothing to you, let
it be nothing to you! I have told you it is somewhat to you, and it
concerns all your religion, and all the good interest of Europe.

I have, thank God, considered; I would beg of you to consider a
little more with me—what that resistance is that is likely to be made
to this mighty torrent that is like to be coming from all parts upon
all Protestants? Who is there that holdeth up his head to oppose

this great design? A poor Prince [Charles X of Sweden]—indeed poor—but a man in his person as gallant and truly, I think I may say, as good as any these late ages have brought forth; a man that adventured his all against the Popish interest in Poland, and made his acquisition still good for the Protestant religion. He is now reduced into a corner: and that addeth to the grief of all, and more than all that hath been spoken before (I wish it may not be too truly said!) that men of our religion forget that and seek his ruin.[4]

And I beseech you consider a little: consider the consequence of that! For doth all this signify? Is it only a noise? Or hath it an articulate sound with it? Men that are not true to that religion we profess—I am persuaded with greater truth, uprighteousness and sincerity than it is by any collected body, so nearly gathered together as these nations are in all the world—God will find them out! I beseech you consider how things do cooperate. If this may seem but to be a design against your well-being? It is against your very being though; this artifice, and this complex design against the Protestant interest—wherein so many Protestants are not so right as were to be wished. If they can shut us out of the Baltic Sea and make themselves masters of that, where is your trade? Where are your materials to preserve your shipping? Or where will you be able to challenge any right by sea or justify yourselves against a foreign invasion in your own soil? Think upon it: this is in design! I do believe if you will go to ask the poor mariner in his red cap and coat as he passeth from ship to ship, you will hardly find in any ship but they will tell you this is designed against you. So obvious is it, by this and other things, that you are the object. And in my conscience I know not for what else but because of the purity of the profession amongst you, who have not yet made it your trade to prefer your profit before your godliness but reckon godliness the greater gain.

But should it so happen that, as your contrivances stand, you should not be able to vindicate yourselves against all whatsoever— I name no other State upon this head, but I think all acknowledge States are engaged in this combination—judge you where you are!

---

[4] For a recent appraisal of Cromwell's attitude toward Charles X of Sweden see Michael Roberts, "Cromwell and the Baltic," in *Essays in Swedish History* (London, 1967).

You have accounted yourselves happy in being environed with a great ditch from all the world beside. Truly you will not be able to keep your ditch nor your shipping unless you turn your ships and shipping into troops of horse and companies of foot and fight to defend yourselves in *terra firma*!

9

Men of Spirit

Cromwell believed in supporting liberty of thought so long as it did not result in anarchy; he also believed in the equality of all Protestant Christians. He judged men by the quality of the service they offered to God and their country. Thus he had no respect for the nobility as such, though he recognized that gentle birth gave an advantage. When he first raised soldiers to fight for what he believed to be the cause of righteousness in the civil war, he sought for men of dedication and spirit.

"GET ME MEN OF A SPIRIT"[1]

I was a person that, from my first employment, was suddenly preferred and lifted up from lesser trusts to greater; from my first being a captain of a troop of horse; and I did labour as well as I could to discharge my trust; and God blessed me, as it pleased Him. And I did truly and plainly—and then in a way of foolish simplicity, as it was judged by very great and wise men, and good men too, desire to make my instruments help me in that work. And I will deal plainly with you: I had a worthy friend then and he was a very noble person, and I know his memory is grateful to you all —Mr. John Hampden.

At my first going out into this engagement, I saw our men were beaten at every hand. I did indeed; and I desired him that he would make some additions to Lord Essex's army, some new regiments; and I told him I would be serviceable to him in bringing such men in as I thought had a spirit that would do something in the work. This is very true that I tell you: God knows I lie not. 'Your troopers," said I, "are most of them old decayed serving men

[1] Speech to Committee at Whitehall, April 13, 1657.

55

and tapsters and such kind of fellows; and," said I, "their troopers [the Royalists] are gentlemen's sons, younger sons and persons of quality; do you think the spirits of such base and mean fellows will be ever able to encounter gentlemen that have honour and courage and resolution in them?" Truly I pressed him in this manner conscientiously; and truly I did tell him: "you must get men of a spirit: and take it not ill what I say—I know you will not—of a spirit that is likely to go on as far as gentlemen will go—or else I am sure you will be beaten still." I told him so; I did truly. He was a wise and worthy person; and he did think I talked a good notion, but an impracticable one.

Truly I told him I could do somewhat in it. I did do so, and truly I may say this to you—impute it to what you please—I raised such men as had the fear of God before them and made some conscience of what they did; and from that day forward, I must say to you, they were never beaten, and wherever they were engaged against the enemy, they beat continuously. . . .

I tell you there are such men in this nation; that are godly men of the same spirit, men that will not be beaten down with worldly or carnal spirit while they keep their integrity.

HONEST AND PLAIN MEN [2]

If you choose godly, honest men to be captains of horse, honest men will follow them; and they will be careful to mount such. . . . I had rather have a plain russet-coated captain that knows what he fights for, and loves what he knows, than that which you call a gentleman and is nothing else. I honour a gentleman that is so indeed. I understand Mr. Margery hath honest men that will follow him; if so, be pleased to make use of him; it much concerns your good to have conscientious men. . . .

Captain Ralph Margery, who served in Cromwell's own regiment, was criticized because his troop requisitioned horses during the fighting in the eastern countries at the opening of

[2] Letter to the Deputy Lieutenants of Suffolk, from Cambridge, September, 1643.

the civil wars. Cromwell then wrote to the Deputy Lieutenants again:

I hear there hath been much exception taken to Captain Margery and his officers for taking of horses. I am sorry you should discountenance those who—not to make benefit to themselves but to serve their country—are willing to venture their lives and to purchase to themselves the displeasure of bad men, that they may do a public benefit. I undertake not to justify all Captain Margery's actions, but his own conscience knows whether he hath taken the horses of any but malignants [Royalists] and it were somewhat too hard to put it upon the consciences of your fellow Deputy Lieutenants whether they have not freed the horses of known malignants; a fault not less, considering the sad estate of this kingdom than to take a horse from a known honest man; the offence being against the public, which is a considerable aggravation. . . .

If these men be accounted troublesome to the county, I shall be glad you would send them all to me. I'll bid them welcome. And when they have fought for you and endured some other difficulties of war which your honester men will hardly bear, I pray you then let them go for honester men. . . . Gentlemen, it may be it provokes some spirits to see such plain men made captains of horse. It had been well that men of honour and birth had entered into these employments, but why do they not appear? Who would have hindered them? But seeing it was necessary the work must go on, better plain men than none, but best to have men patient of wants, faithful and conscientious in the employment, and such, I hope, these will [ap]prove themselves to be. . . .[3]

THE STATE TAKES NO NOTICE OF OPINIONS [4]

Sir, the State in choosing men to serve them takes no notice of their opinions, if they be willing faithfully to serve them, that satisfies. I advised you formerly to bear with men of different minds from yourself: if you had done it when I advised you to it, I think

[3] Letter of September 28, 1643.
[4] Letter to Major-General Crawford, March 10, 1643.

you would not have had so many stumbling blocks in your way. It
may be you judge otherwise, but I tell you my mind. I desire you
would receive this man [Lieutenant-Colonel Henry Warner, who
was apparently an Anabaptist serving under a Presbyterian Major-
General] into your favour and good opinion. I believe, if he follow my counsel, he will deserve no other but respect from you.
Take heed of being sharp, or too easily sharpened by others,
against those to whom you can object little but that they square not
with you in every opinion concerning matters of religion. . . .

"HE THAT PRAYS BEST WILL FIGHT BEST" [5]

Indeed I was not satisfied with your last speech to me about
[Captain] Empson, that he was a better preacher than a fighter, or
words to that effect. Truly I think he that prays and preaches best
will fight best. I know nothing will give courage and confidence as
the knowledge of God in Christ will; and I bless God to see any in
this army able and willing to impart the knowledge they have for
the good of others.

[5] Letter to Colonel Francis Hacker, December 25, 1650.

10
Cromwell as Lord Protector

Cromwell was appointed Lord Protector under the terms of the Instrument of Government in December, 1653, and met his first Protectorate parliament in September, 1654. Here are some extracts from his speech when Parliament opened: he justified his position as being the means of putting an end to anarchy and restoring internal peace.

"REMEDYING A HEAP OF CONFUSIONS"[1]

You are met here on the greatest occasion that I believe England ever saw; having upon your shoulders the interests of three great nations with the territories belonging to them—and truly, I believe I may say it without hyperbole, you have upon your shoulders the interest of all the Christian people in the world. And the expectation is that I should let you know (as far as I have cognizance of it) the occasion of your assembling together at this time. . . .

After so many changes and turnings, which this nation hath laboured under—to have such a day of hope as this is, and such a door of hope opened by God to us, truly I believe, some months since would have been above our thoughts!—I confess it would have been worthy of such a meeting as this is to have remembered that which was the rise and gave the first beginning to all those turnings and tossings which have been upon these nations: and to have given you a series of transactions—not of men, but of the Providence of God, all along unto our late changes: as also to the ground of our first undertaking to oppose that usurpation and tyranny that was upon us both in civils and spirituals: and the several grounds particularly applicable to the several changes that

[1] Speech of September 4, 1654.

59

have been. But I have two or three reasons which divert me from such a way of proceeding at this time.

If I should have gone in that way, that which is upon my heart to have said (which is written there that if I would blot it out I could not) would have spent this day: the providences and dispensations of God have been so stupendous. . . .

That which I judge to be the end of your meeting, the great end, [is] healing and settling. . . .

Howbeit I think it will be more than necessary to let you know (at least as well as I may) in what condition this, nay, these nations were when this Government was undertaken. . . .

What was our condition? Every man's hand (almost) was against his brother—at least his heart; little regarding anything that should cement and might have a tendency in it to cause us to grow into one. All the dispensations of God, His terrible ones, He having met us in the way of His judgment in a ten-years civil war, a very sharp one; His merciful dispensations they did not work upon us! But we had our humours and interests—and indeed I fear our humours were more than our interests. And certainly, as it fell out, in such cases our passions were more than our judgments. Was not everything (almost) grown arbitrary? Who knew how or where to have right without some obstructions or other intervening? Indeed we were almost grown arbitrary in everything.

What was the face that was upon our affairs as to the interest of the nation; to the authority of the nation; to the magistracy; to the ranks and orders of men, whereby England hath been known for hundreds of years? A nobleman, a gentleman, a yeoman: that is a good interest of the nation and a great one! The magistracy of the nation, was it not almost trampled under foot, under despite and contempt by men of Levelling principles? I beseech you, for the orders of men and ranks of men, did not that Levelling principle tend to the reducing of all to an equality? Did it think to do so? Or did it practise towards it for property and interest? What was the purport of it but to make the tenant as liberal a fortune as the landlord? Which, I think, if obtained, would not have lasted long! The men of that principle after they had served their own turns would have cried up interest and property then fast enough! This instance is instead of many. And that this thing did extend far is manifest; because it was a pleasing voice to all poor men, and truly not unwelcome to all bad men. . . .

Indeed in spiritual things the case was more sad and deplorable. . . . The prodigious blasphemies; contempt of God and Christ, denying of Him, contempt of Him and His ordinances, and of the Scriptures. . . .

And although these things will not be owned publicly as to practice (they being so abominable and odious); yet how this principle [of wantonness] extends itself, and whence it had its rise makes me think of a second sort of men who, it's true, as I said, will not practise nor own these things, yet can tell the magistrate that he hath nothing to do with men thus holding [such principles]: for these are matters of conscience and opinion: they are matters of religion; what hath the magistrate to do with these things? He is to look to the outward man but not to look to the inward. And truly it so happens that though these things do break out visibly to all, yet the principle wherewith these things are carried on so forbids the magistrate to meddle with them, as it hath hitherto kept offenders from punishment.

Such considerations and pretensions of liberty, what are they leading us towards! Liberty of conscience and liberty of subjects— two as glorious things to be contended for as any God hath given us; yet both these also abused for the patronising of villainies; insomuch as that it hath been an ordinary thing to say, and in dispute to affirm, that it was not in the magistrate's power: he hath nothing to do with it. . . .

The axe was laid at the root of the ministry. It was antiChristian, it was Babylonish [it was said]. It suffered under such a judgment, that the truth of it is, as the extremity was great according to the former system, I wish it prove not as great on this hand. The extremity was that no man, though he had never so good a testimony, though he had received gifts from Christ, might preach unless [he was] ordained. So now many affirm, on the other hand, that he who is ordained hath a nullity or antiChristianism stamped upon his calling: so that he ought not to preach or be heard. I wish it may not too, too justly be said that there was severity and sharpness, yea too much of an imposing spirit in matter of conscience, a spirit unChristian enough in any times, most unfit for these: denying liberty to those who have earned it with their blood; who have gained civil liberty and religious also, for those who would thus impose upon them.

We may reckon among these our spiritual evils, an evil that hath more refinedness in it, and more colour for it, and hath deceived more people of integrity than the rest have done; for few have been catched with the former mistakes but such as have apostatised from their holy profession, such as being corrupt in their consciences have been forsaken by God, and left to such noisome opinions. But, I say, there is another error of more refined sort; which many honest people whose hearts are sincere, many of them belonging to God [have fallen into] and that is the mistaken notion of Fifth Monarchy [the belief in the imminent coming of Christ and that in the meantime his Saints should rule on earth] . . .

Indeed this is that which doth most declare the danger of the spirit. For if these were but notions—I mean the instances that I have given you both of civil and spiritual [doctrines], if I say they were but notions, they were to be left alone. Notions will hurt none but them that have them. But when they come to such practices as to tell us that liberty and property are not the badges of the Kingdom of Christ; when they tell us not that we are to regulate law, but that law is to be abrogated, indeed subverted; and perhaps wish to bring in the Judaical law instead of our known laws settled among us: this is worthy of every magistrate's consideration. Especially where every stone is turned to bring confusion. I think, I say, this will be worthy of the magistrate's consideration. . . .

These things being thus—as I am persuaded it is not hard to convince every person here they were thus—what a heap of confusions were upon these poor nations! And either things must have been left to sink into miseries these premises would suppose or a remedy must be applied. A remedy hath been applied: that hath been this Government: a thing I shall say very little unto. The thing is open and visible to be seen and read by all men; and therefore let it speak for itself. Only let me say this—because I can speak with comfort and confidence before a Greater than you all, that is before the Lord: that in the intention of it, as to the approving our hearts to God (let men judge as they please), it is calculated for the interest of the people—for the interest of the people alone and for their good without respect to any other interest. . . .

It [the Government] hath had some things in desire; and it hath done some things actually [that is, reforming the laws and settling religion]. One thing more this Government hath done: it hath been instrumental to call a free parliament—which, blessed be God, we see here this day. I say, a free parliament. And that it may continue so, I hope is in the heart and spirit of every good man in England—save such discontented persons as I have formerly mentioned. It's that which as I have desired above my life, I shall desire to keep it so, above my life. . . .

We are thus far, through the mercy of God. We have cause to take notice of it, that we are not brought into misery, but [have] a door of hope open. And I may say this to you: if the Lord's blessing and His presence go along with the management of affairs at this meeting you will be enabled to put the topstone to this work and make the nation happy. But this must be by knowing the true state of affairs; that you are yet, like the people under circumcision, but raw. Your peaces are but newly made. And it's a maxim not to be despised: "Though peace be made, yet it's interest that keeps peace"; and I hope you will trust it no further than you see interest upon it. And therefore I wish you may go forward and not backward; and that you may have the blessings of God upon your endeavours. It's one of the great ends of calling this parliament that this ship of the Commonwealth may be brought into a safe harbour; which, I assure you, it will not well be, without your counsel and advice. . . .

"I CALLED NOT MYSELF TO THIS PLACE" [2]

In his second speech to the first Protectorate parliament Cromwell outlined how the "Instrument of Government," the written constitution under which his Protectorate functioned, had come into being. He described the confusion that followed the Parliamentary victory in the civil wars, the attempt of the remnant of King Charles's "Long Parliament"

[2] Speech of September 12, 1654.

("the Rump") *to perpetuate itself as executive and legislative*
power combined, the overthrow of the Rump by the army,
the calling together by the army of a nominated "Assembly
of Saints" to frame a new constitution, and the giving back
of political power into the hands of himself as commander-
in-chief until he voluntarily abandoned military government
after the setting up of the Protectorate.

"That I called not myself to this place" is my first assertion.
"That I bear not witness to myself, but have many witnesses" is
my second. These are the two things I shall take the liberty to
speak more fully to you of—to make plain and clear that which
I have said, I must take liberty to look back.

I was by birth a gentleman; living neither in any considerable
height nor yet in obscurity. I have been called to several employments in the nation: to serve in parliaments; and (because I would
not be over-tedious) I did endeavour to discharge the duty of an
honest man in those services, to God and His people's interest and
[that] of the Commonwealth; having, when time was, a competent
acceptance in the hearts of men and some evidences thereof. . . .

I, having had some occasions to see (together with my brethren
and countrymen) a happy period put to our sharp wars and contests
with the then common enemy, hoped in a private capacity to have
reaped the fruit and the benefit, together with my brethren, of
our hard labours and hazards: to wit, the enjoyment of peace and
liberty and the privileges of a Christian and of a man, in some
equality with others, according as it should please God to dispense
unto me. And when, I say, God had put an end to our wars, at
least brought them to a very hopeful issue, very near an end (after
Worcester fight) I came up to London to pay my service and duty
to the Parliament that then sat, and hoping that all minds would
have been disposed to answer that which seemed to be the mind of
God, namely, to give peace and rest to His people, and especially
to those who had bled more than others in the carrying on of the
military affairs, I was much disappointed in my expectation. For
this issue did not prove so. Whatever may be boasted or misrepre-
sented, it was not so, not so! . . .

I pressed the Parliament, as a member, to period themselves once and again, and again, and ten and twenty times over. I told them (for I knew it better than any one man in the parliament could know it; because of my manner of life, which had led me everywhere up and down the nation, thereby giving me to see and know the temper and spirits of all men, the best of men) that the nation loathed their sitting. I knew it. And, so far as I could discern, when they were dissolved, there was not much as the barking of a dog, or any general and visible repining at it! . . .

And that there was high cause for their dissolving is most evident: not only in regard there was a just fear of the parliament perpetuating themselves, but because it was their design. And had not their heels been trod upon by importunities from abroad, even to threats, I believe there would never have been thought of rising or going out of that room, to the world's end. I myself was sounded and by no mean persons tempted; and addresses were made me to that very end: that parliament might have been thus perpetuated; that the vacant places might be supplied by new elections; and so continue from generation to generation.

I have declined, I have declined very much, to open these things to you. Yet, having proceeded thus far, I must tell you that poor men, under this arbitrary power, were driven, like flocks of sheep, by forty in a morning; to the confiscation of goods and estates; without any man being able to give a reason that two of them had deserved to forfeit a shilling! I tell you the truth. And my soul, and many persons whose faces I see in this place, were exceedingly grieved at these things; and knew not which way to help it but by their mournings and giving their negatives when occasions served. I have given you but a taste of miscarriages. . . . It's true this will be said, that there was remedy endeavoured: to put an end to this perpetual parliament by giving us a future representative. How that was gotten, by what importunities it was obtained, and how unwillingly yielded unto, is well known.

What was the remedy? It was a seeming willingness to give us successive parliaments. What was that succession? It was that when one parliament had left its seat, another was to sit down immediately in the room thereof, without any caution to avoid what was the danger, namely perpetuating of the same parliaments. Which is a sore, now, that will ever be running, so long as men are ambitious and troublesome, if a due remedy be not found.

Nay, at best what will such a remedy amount to? It is a conversion of a parliament that should have been and was perpetual to a legislative power always sitting. And so the liberties and interests and lives of people not judged by any certain laws and power, but by an arbitrary power, which is incident and necessary to parliaments. By an arbitrary power, I say: to make men's estates liable to confiscation and their persons to imprisonment, sometimes by laws made after the fact committed; often by taking the judgment both in capital and criminal things to themselves, who in former times were not known to exercise such a judicature. This, I suppose, was the case. And, in my opinion, the remedy was fitted to the disease, especially coming in the rear of a parliament so exercising the power and authority as this had done but immediately before.

Truly, I confess upon these grounds and with the satisfaction of divers other persons, seeing nothing could be had otherwise, the parliament was dissolved: we, desiring to see if a few might have been called together for some short time who might put the nation into some way of certain settlement, did call those gentlemen out of the several parts of the nation for that purpose [the Assembly of Saints]. . . . I say that as a principal end in calling that Assembly was the settlement of the nation, so a chief end to myself was that I might have the opportunity to lay down the power which was in my hands. I say to you again in the presence of that God who hath blessed and been with me in all my adversities and success: that was, as to myself, my greatest end—a desire perhaps and, I am afraid, sinful enough, to be quit of the power God had most clearly by His Providence put into my hand before He called me to lay it down, and before those honest ends of our fighting were attained and settled. I say, the authority I had in my hand being so boundless as it was—for by act of parliament, I was General of all the forces in the three nations of England, Scotland and Ireland—in which unlimited condition I did not desire to live a day—we called that meeting for the ends before expressed.

What the event and issue of that meeting was, we may sadly remember. It hath much teaching in it, and I hope will make us all wiser for the future. But this meeting [not] succeeding . . . and giving such a disappointment to our hopes, I shall not now make any repetition thereof: only the result was that they came and brought to me a parchment, signed by very much the major part of them, expressing their resigning and redelivery of the power and authority that was committed to them back again into my hands. And I can say it, in the presence of divers persons here, that do know whether I lie in that, that I did not know one tittle of that resignation until they all came and brought it and delivered it into my hands. Of this there are also in this presence many witnesses. I received this resignation; having formerly used my endeavours and persuasions to keep them together. Observing their differences, I thought it my duty to give advices to them, that so I might prevail with them for union. But it had the effect that I told you; and I had my disappointment.

When this proved so, we were exceedingly to seek how to settle things for the future. My power again, by this resignation, was as boundless and unlimited as before; all things being subjected to arbitrariness and a person having power over the three nations, without bound or limit set; and upon the matter, all government dissolved; all civil administrations at an end, as will presently appear.

The gentlemen that undertook to frame this [scheme of] government did consult divers days together how to frame somewhat that might give us settlement. They did consult, and that I was not privy to their councils they know it. When they had finished their model in some measure, or made a very good preparation of it it became communicative. They told me that except I would undertake the government, they thought things would hardly come to a composure and settlement, but blood and confusion would break in upon us. I refused it again and again, as God and those persons know; . . . I confess after many arguments they urging on me that I did not receive anything that put me into any higher capacity than I was in before, but that it limited me and bound my hands to act nothing to the prejudice of the nations without consent of a Council, until the parliament [met] and then limited by the parliament, as the act of government [i.e., "the Instrument"] expresseth,—I did accept it.

I might repeat this again to you, if it were needful, but I hardly think it is: I was arbitrary in power; having the armies in the three nations under my command; and truly not very ill beloved by them, nor very ill beloved then by the people; by the good people. And I believe I should have been more beloved if they had known the truth, as things were, before God and in themselves, and before divers of these gentlemen whom I but now mentioned unto you. I did, at the entreaty of divers persons of honour and quality, at the entreaty of very many of the chief officers of the army then present, and at their request I did accept of the place and title of Protector: and was in the presence of the Commissioners of the Seal, the judges, the Lord Mayor and Aldermen of the City of London, the soldiery, divers gentlemen, citizen and divers other people and persons of quality, and so forth, accompanied to Westminster Hall, where I took my oath to this Government. This was not done in a corner: it was open and public. This Government hath been exercised by a Council with a desire to be faithful in all things—and amongst other trusts, to be faithful in calling this parliament. . . .

[After outlining the "four fundamentals" (see page 32 above), Cromwell demanded that the members of the first Protectorate parliament should give their assent to them.]

The "[Instrument of] Government" doth declare that you have a legislative power without a negative from me. And the "[Instrument of] Government" doth express you may make any laws; and if I give not my consent within twenty days to the passing your laws, they are *ipso facto* laws, whether I consent or no, if not contrary to the "[Instrument of] Government." You have an absolute legislative power in all things that can possibly concern the good and interest of the public; and I think you may make these nations happy by this settlement. And I, for my part, shall be willing to be bound more than I am in any thing that I may be convinced or may be for the good of the people in preservation of the cause and interest so long contended for.

11
Security

After the dissolution of Cromwell's first Protectorate parliament, the Royalists attempted an uprising in the spring of 1655. Although it was suppressed without much difficulty, the government felt it necessary to strengthen internal security by organized policing. A horse militia was enlisted in various groups of counties, or "associations," under the command of major-generals, to support, though not to supersede, the existing local authorities. This was a temporary security measure, which sometimes has been inaccurately described as a military dictatorship. It seems to have owed its inspiration to Major-General John Lambert and its Puritan aspects to Cromwell. But Cromwell never was entirely happy about it, though he defended the arrangements before the authorities of the City of London and the second Protectorate parliament. To pay for the upkeep of the horse militia, a special levy was imposed upon known Royalists, a property tax of 10 per cent, which was therefore known as the "decimation."

"THE PEACE OF THE NATION" [1]

His Highness on Wednesday last [March 5, 1656] was near two hours in delivering a speech at Whitehall to the Lord Mayor's Court of Aldermen and Common Council of London: wherein he told them that since fair means would not indulge, foul should enforce the Royal party to peaceable deportment; and seeing they were the cause (by their late eruption) of raising militia troops to preserve the peace of the nation, it was thought reasonable that their estate should only be charged therewith, that so they might be in the nature of a standing militia, and yet not to warfare at

[1] *Public Intelligencer*, March 3–10, 1656.

69

their own charge, being at all times to be drawn forth upon occasion; that the soldiers as well as the officers were so many inhabitants of each association under their respective major-generals, and would thereby fitly serve to be so many watchmen or spies to give notice of or apprehend such as were of dissolute lives and conversation, who lived like gentlemen and yet had no visible way for the same, being cheaters and the like, who were more fit to be sent beyond the seas than to remain here.

That God Almighty hath given us many blessings and deliverances, and now seemingly brought us into a probability of enjoying peace, which called upon us to make some returns thereof, by endeavouring that after all our expense of blood and treasure, the same might reap some fruits thereof. And this way the Lord hath owned by making more effectual than was expected, and by receiving a good acceptation with those who of late stood at some distance with us, so that the sole end of this way of procedure was the security of the peace of the nation, [and] the suppressing of vice and encouragement of virtue—the very end of magistracy.

That there was a remissness in some of the Justices of the Peace by many of whom company keeping etc. was countenanced, but now that noblemen, gentlemen and all ranks and qualities must give security for their peaceable and civil deportment or go to prison. That we had indeed many and good laws, yet that we have lived rather under the name and notion of law than under the thing, so that 'tis resolved to regulate the same (God assisting) oppose who will. That now the Major-Generals had gone through all the counties of England and Wales, and where the Major-Generals were present in action those loose and vagrant persons did fly thence to other counties, the Major-Generals' occasions not permitting them to be in action [everywhere] at on time. And for that [matter] this city was a place that gave shelter to many such idle, loose persons, who had and have their recourse thereto, the same practice is intended to be set on foot in the city by their Major-General Skippon, the Lieutenant of the Tower, and others commissioned with him; and therefore His Highness thought fit to acquaint the Lord Mayor and these gentlemen present with the same, to the end no misunderstanding may be had thereof, for that thereby the good government of the city is intended, and not at all to supersede them, or at least to diminish any of their rights, privileges or liberties. . . .

"PERSONS OF KNOWN INTEGRITY" [2]

I am to tell you, by the way, a word to justify a thing [the Major-Generals] that, I hear, is much spoken of. When we knew all these designs before mentioned; when we found that the Cavaliers would not be quiet . . . truly when this insurrection was, and we saw it in all the roots and grounds of it, we did find out a little poor invention, which I hear has been much regretted. . . . I say, there was a little thing invented, which was the erecting of your Major-Generals: to have a little inspection upon the people thus divided, thus discontented, thus dissatisfied, in divers interests by the Popish party. The Lord Taafe and others [exiled Royalists] the most consisting of natural-Irish rebels, and all those men we have fought against in Ireland, and expulsed from thence, as having had a hand in that bloody massacre of those that were under his power; who should have joined in this excellent business of insurrection!

And upon such a rising as that was, truly I think if ever anything were justifiable as to necessity, and honest in every respect, this was. And I could as soon venture my life with it as anything I ever undertook! We did find out—I mean myself and the Council— that if there were need to have greater forces to carry on this work, it was a most righteous thing to put the charge upon that party which was the cause of it. And if there be any man that hath a face looking averse to this, I dare pronounce him to be a man against the interest of England. Upon this account, and upon this ground of necessity when we saw what game they were upon and knew individual persons—and of the greatest rank not a few— engaged in this business . . . and by letters intercepted which made it as clear as the day—we did think it our duty to make that class of persons, whom as evident as anything in the world, were in combination, bear their shares of the charge one with another for the raising of the forces that were so necessary to defend us against those designs. And truly if any man be angry at it, I am plain and shall use a homely expression: "Let him turn the buckle of his

[2] Speech to Parliament, September 17, 1656.

girdle behind him!" If this were to be done again, I would do it.

How the Major-Generals have behaved themselves in that work? I hope they are men, as to their persons, of known integrity and fidelity and men that have ventured their blood and lives for that good cause—if it be thought such, as it was well stated against all the humours and fancies of men! And truly England doth yet receive one day more of lengthening-out its tranquillity by that same service of theirs.

Well; your danger is as you have seen. And truly I am sorry it is so great. I wish it might cause no despondency, as truly, I think, it will not: because we are Englishmen; that is of good account. And if God give a nation the property of valour and courage, it is honour and mercy and much more. Because you all, I hope, are Christian men, Christian men that know Jesus Christ and know the cause that hath been mentioned to you this day.

"TIME TO SET ASIDE ARBITRARY PROCEEDINGS" [3]

At the end of January, 1657, a Militia Bill, sponsored by the Major-Generals was defeated in the second Protectorate parliament. During the debates about it, one speaker said its object was "to cantonize the nation and prostitute our laws and civil peace to a power that was never set up in any nation without dangerous consequences." Cromwell recognized its unpopularity and blamed the Major-Generals for the rebuff or "foil."

They had made him their drudge upon all occasions: to dissolve the Long Parliament, who had contracted evil enough by long sitting; to call a parliament or convention of their naming [the Assembly of Saints] who met; and what did they? Fly at liberty and property, insomuch as if one man who had twelve cows, they held another that wanted cows ought to take a share with his neighbour. Who could have said any thing was their own if they had gone on? After their dissolution how was I pressed by you for the rooting out of the ministry; nay, rather than fail, to starve them out. A

---

[3] Address to meeting of army officers, February 27, 1657.

parliament was afterwards called. They sat for five months; it is true we hardly heard of them in all that time. They took the Instrument [of Government] into debate and they must needs be dissolved: and yet stood not the Instrument in need of mending? Was not the case hard with me to be put upon to swear to that which was so hard to be kept?

Some time after that you thought it was necessary to have Major-Generals and the first rise to that motion then was the late general insurrections and was justifiable; and you Major-Generals did your part well. You might have gone on. Who bid you go to the House [of Commons] with a Bill and there receive a foil?

After you had exercised this power a while, impatient were you till a parliament was called. I gave my vote against it, but you [were] confident by your own strength and interest to get men chosen to your heart's desire. How you have failed therein, and how much the country hath been disobliged, is well known. That it is time to come to a settlement and lay aside arbitrary proceedings, so unacceptable to the nation. And by the proceedings of this parliament, you see they stand in need of a check or balancing power (meaning the House of Lords or House so constituted) for the case of James Naylor [a Quaker severely punished for blasphemy by vote of the Commons] might happen to be your case. By their judicial power, they fall upon life and member [limb] and doth the Instrument enable me to control it?

12
Kingship

The failure of the constitution known as the Instrument of Government to provide a workable political settlement and the subsequent necessity of strengthening internal security by the unpopular system of Major-Generals induced the majority of Cromwell's second parliament to draw up a new constitution known as the Petition and Advice. It provided for a two-chamber legislature, a new system of church government, and an executive authority headed by Cromwell, who was to have the title of King, instead of Lord Protector. Cromwell liked the idea of the new constitution, but hesitated about accepting the title of King. He thought it was a mere flourish, a "feather in his cap," though he realized that the kingship was a traditional foundation of law and order. He finally refused the title, but accepted the rest of the proposed constitution.

"THE TWO GREATEST CONCERNMENTS" [1]

I have, as well as I could, taken into consideration of the things contained in the paper [or draft constitution] which was presented to me by the parliament in the banqueting house on Tuesday last; and sought of God that I might return such an answer as might become me and be worthy of parliament. I must needs bears this testimony to them that they have been zealous of the two greatest concernments that God hath in the world: the one is that of religion and of the preservation of the professors of it to give them all due and just liberty and to assert the truths of God —which you have done in this paper; and do refer it to be done more fully by yourselves and me. And as to liberty of men professing godliness under a variety of forms amongst us you have done

[1] Speech to Parliamentary deputation, April 3, 1657.

74

that which was never done before. And I pray God it may not fall upon the people of God as a fault in them if they do not put such a value upon this that is done as never was put on anything since Christ's time for such a catholic interest of the People of God.

The other thing cared for is the civil liberty and interest of the nation. Which though it is, and I think ought to be, subordinate to a more peculiar interest of God—yet it is the next best God hath given men in this world; and if well, it is better than any rock to fence men in their own interests. Then if any one whatsoever think the interest of Christians and the interest of the nation inconsistent, I wish my soul would never enter into their secrets!

These are things I must acknowledge Christian and honourable; and are provided for by you like Christians, even men of honour— and English men. And to this I must and shall bear testimony, while I live, against all gainsayers whatsoever. And upon these two interests, if God shall account me worthy, I shall live and die. And I must say, if I were to give an account before a greater tribunal than any earthly one; and if I were asked, why I have engaged all along in the late war, I could give no answer but it would be a wicked one if it did not comprehend these two ends. Only give me leave to say, and to say it seriously (the issue will prove it so) that you have one or two considerations that do stick with me. The one is you have named me by another title than that I now bear.

You do necessitate my answer to be categorical; and you have left me without a liberty of choice as to all. I question not your wisdom in doing of it; but think myself obliged to acquiesce in your determination, knowing you are men of wisdom, and considering the trust you are under. It is a duty not to question the reason of any thing you have done.

I should be very brutish should I not acknowledge the exceeding high honour and respect you have had for me in this paper. Truly, according to what the world calls good, it hath all good in it—according to the worldly comprehension of sovereign power. You have testified your value and affection as to my person as high as you could; for more you could not do. I hope I shall always keep a grateful memory of this in my heart; and by you I return [to] the parliament my grateful acknowledgement. Whatever other men's thoughts may be, I shall not own ingratitude. But I must needs say that that may be fit for you to offer which may not be fit for me to undertake. . . .

KINGSHIP "CONVENIENT BUT NOT NECESSARY" [2]

To return some answer to the things that were so ably and well said the other day on behalf of the parliament's putting that title [King] into the instrument of settlement. . . .

Your arguments, which I say, were chiefly upon the law, seem to carry with them a great deal of necessary conclusiveness to enforce that one thing of kingship. And if your arguments come upon me to enforce upon me the ground of necessity—why then I have no room to answer; for what must be, must be. And therefore I did reckon it of my business to consider, whether there was such a necessity, or would arise such a necessity from those arguments.

It was said "that kingship is not a title, but an office, so interwoven with the fundamental laws of the nation that they cannot, or cannot well, be executed and exercised without [it]—partly, if I may say so, upon a supposed ignorance which the law hath of any other title. It knows no other; neither doth any other know it, the reciprocation is such. This title or name or office, as you were pleased to say, is understood in the dimensions of it, in the powers and prerogatives of it, which are by the law made certain; and the law cannot tell when it [kingship?] keeps within compass and when it exceeds its limits. And the law knowing this, the people can know it also. And the people to love what they know. And it will be neither *pro salute populi* nor for our safety to obtrude upon them names that they do not and cannot understand." . . .

I cannot take upon me to repel these grounds; for they are strong and rational. But if I shall be able to make any answer to them, I must not grant that they are necessarily conclusive; but take them only as arguments that have perhaps much of conveniency and probability towards conclusiveness.

[2] Speech to Parliamentary committee, April 13, 1657.

Truly, though kingship be not a title, but a name of office that runs through the law; yet it is not so *ratione nominis* from the reason of the name but from what is signified. It is a name of office plainly implying the supreme authority: it is no more; nor can it be stretched to more . . .

I had rather, if I were to choose, if it were the original question —which I hope is altogether out of the question—I had rather have any name from parliament than any other name without it: so much do I think of the authority of parliament. And I believe that all men are of my mind in that; I believe the nation is very much of my mind—though that be an uncertain way of arguing what mind they are of. . . .

What the parliament settles is that which will run through the law; and will lead the thread of government through the land. . . . And if so, then, under favour to me, I think all these arguments from the law . . . are not necessary but are to be understood upon the account of conveniency. It is in your power to dispose and settle. . . .

I am a man standing in the place I am in, which place I undertook not so much out of the hope of doing any good as out of a desire to prevent mischief and evil which I did see was imminent in the nation. I saw we were running headlong into confusion and disorder and would necessarily run into blood; and I was passive to those that desired me to undertake the place I now have. . . . But I profess I had not that apprehension, when I undertook the place, that I could do much good, but I did think I might prevent imminent evil. And therefore I am not contending for one name compared with another; and therefore have nothing to answer to any arguments that were used in giving preference to Kingship or Protectorship. For I should think that any name were better than my name; and I should think any person fitter than I am for any such business: and I compliment not, God knows it!

But this I would say: that I do think from my very heart you, in settling of the peace and liberties of this nation, which cries as loud upon you as ever nation did for somewhat that may beget a consistence [should aim for this], otherwise the nation will fall to pieces. And in that, as far as I can, I am ready to serve not as a King, but as a Constable. For truly I have, as before God, thought it often that I could not tell what my business was, nor what I was in the place I stood, save comparing myself to a good constable to keep the peace of the parish. And truly this hath been my content and satisfaction in the troubles that I have undergone—that yet you have peace. . . .

Truly the providences of God hath laid aside this title [of king] providentially *de facto*: and this not by sudden humour or passion; but it hath been by issue of as great deliberation as ever was in a nation. It hath been the issue of ten or twelve years civil war wherein much blood hath been shed. I will not dispute the justice of it when it was done; nor need I now tell you that my opinion is in the case were it *de novo* to be done. But if it be at all disputable; and that a man comes and finds that God in His severity hath not only eradicated a whole family, and thrust them out of the land, for reasons best known to Himself, but hath made the issue and close of it to be the very eradication of a Name or Title—which *de facto* is, it was not done by me nor by them that tendered me the Government that I now act in: it was done by the Long Parliament . . . And God hath seemed providentially not only to strike at the Family but at the Name. . . .

I beseech you think not that I bring this as an argument to prove anything. God hath seemed so to deal with the Persons and with the Family [that is, Charles I and Charles II] that He blasted the Title. . . . I will not seek to set up that, that Providence hath destroyed and laid in the dust: and I would not build Jericho again! And this is somewhat to me and to my judgment and conscience. That is true, it is that that hath an awe upon my spirit. And I must confess, as the times are—they are very fickle, very uncertain, nay God knows you had need have a great deal of faith to strengthen you in your work, and all assistance; you had need to look at settlement—I would rather I were in my grave than hinder you in anything that may be for settlement for the nation. For the nation needs it, and never needed it more. And therefore out of the love and honour I bear you, I am forever bound to do, whatever becomes of me, [what is best for that]. . . .

"AT BEST I SHOULD DO IT DOUBTINGLY" [8]

After long discussions about the proposed new scheme of government, Cromwell finally refused the title of King.

I must confess therefore that though I do acknowledge all the other particulars, yet I must be a little confident in this—that what with the circumstances of time or persons, whether circumstances that relate to the whole or private particular circumstances that compass any person that is to render an account of his own actions—I have truly thought and do still think that if I should, at the best, do anything on this account to answer your expectation [accepting the title of King] I should do it doubtingly. And certainly what is so is not of the faith. And whatsoever is not so, whatsoever is not of faith is sin to him that doth it—whether it be with relation to the substance of the action about which that consideration is conversant, or whether to circumstances about it which make all indifferent actions good or evil. I say "circumstances"; and truly I mean good or evil to him that doth it. . . .

Truly this is my answer: and although I think the [scheme of] Government doth consist of very excellent parts, in all but in that one thing, the title, I should not be an honest man if I should not tell you that I cannot accept of the Government nor undertake the trouble and charge of it—which I have a little more experimented than everybody what troubles and difficulties do befall men under such trusts and in such undertakings. . . . I say I am persuaded to return the answer to you that I cannot undertake this Government with that title of King. And that is mine answer to this great and weighty business.

[8] Speech to Parliamentary committee, May 8, 1657.

13
Cromwell's Prayer[1]

Although this prayer, reported by contemporaries to have been made by Cromwell on his deathbed, may not be completely authentic, there is reason to believe it embodied the essential feelings of the dying man:

Lord, though I am a miserable and wretched creature, I am in Covenant with Thee through Grace. And I may, I will, come to Thee, for Thy People. Thou hast made me, though very unworthy, a mean instrument to do them some good and Thee service; and many of them have set too high a value upon me, though others wish and would be glad of my death.

Lord, however Thou do dispose of me, continue and go on to do good for them. Give them consistency of judgment, one heart, and mutual love; and go on to deliver them, and with the work of reformation; and make the name of Christ glorious in the world.

Teach those who look too much on Thy instruments to depend more upon Thyself. Pardon such as desire to trample upon the dust of a poor worm, for they are Thy People too. And pardon the folly of this short prayer—even for Jesus Christ's sake. And give us a good night, if this be Thy pleasure.

Amen

[1] Charles Harvey, *A Collection of Several Passages* (1659), pp. 11–12.

CROMWELL VIEWED BY HIS CONTEMPORARIES

Men at the top do not have many friends. There is not a vast amount of strictly contemporary material about Cromwell, and most of it, though not all, comes from men who were his critics or enemies. We do not possess any considered judgments about his character even from the diplomatic representatives in London. Much of what they wrote was ephemeral and inaccurate. That is why in portraying Cromwell's personality and ideas, historians have had to rely more upon his own letters and speeches than upon the evidence of other people. Even his closest intimates, such as John Thurloe, his Secretary of State, reported only upon his passing moods.

SIR PHILIP WARWICK: DESIGNED FOR EXTRAORDINARY THINGS [1]

Warwick was a Royalist member of Parliament.

I have no mind to give an ill character of Cromwell; for in his conversation towards me he was ever friendly; 'tho at the latter end of the day finding me ever incorrigible, and having some inducements to suspect me a tamperer, he was sufficiently rigid. The first time that I ever took notice of him was in the very beginning of the parliament held in November, 1640, when I vainly thought myself a courtly young gentleman: (for we courtiers valued ourselves much upon our good clothes). I came one morning into the House well clad, and perceived a gentleman speaking (whom I knew not) very ordinarily apparelled; for it was a plain cloth suit, which seemed to have been made by an ill country tailor; his linen

[1] Philip Warwick, *Memoirs of the Reign of King Charles I* (1702), pp. 247–50.

was plain, and not very clean; and I remember a speck or two of blood upon his little band, which was not much larger than his collar; his hat was without a hat band: his stature was of a good size, his sword stuck close to his side, his countenance swollen and reddish, his voice sharp and untunable, and his eloquence full of fervour; for the subject matter would not bear much of reason; it being in behalf of a servant of Mr Prynne's [John Lilburne] who had dispersed libels against the Queen for her dancing and such like innocent and courtly sports; and he aggravated the imprisonment of this man by the Council Table unto that height that one would have believed the very Government itself had been in great danger by it.

I sincerely profess it lessened much my reverence unto that great council; for he was very much hearkened unto. And yet I lived to see this very gentleman, whom out of no ill will to him I thus describe, by multiplied good successes and real (but usurped) power (having had a better tailor and more converse among good company) in my own eye when for six weeks together I was a prisoner in his serjeant's hands and daily waited at Whitehall, appear of great and majestic deportment and comely presence. Of him therefore I will say no more but that I verily believe he was extraordinarily designed for those extraordinary things, which one while most wickedly and facinorously he acted, and at another as successfully and greatly performed.

After the rendition of Oxford, I living some time with the Lady Beadle (my wife's sister) near Huntingdon, had occasion to converse with Mr Cromwell's physician, Dr Simcott, who assured me that for many years his patient was a most splenetic man, and had fancies about the cross in that town; and that he had been called up to him at midnight and such unseasonable hours very many times, upon such a strong fancy, which made him believe that he was then dying; and there went a story of him that in the daytime lying melancholy in his bed, he believed that a spirit appeared to him, and told him that he should be the greatest man (not mentioning the word King) in this kingdom. Which his uncle, Sir Thomas Steward, who left him all the little estate Cromwell had, told him was traitorous to relate.

The first years of his manhood were spent in a dissolute course of life, in good fellowship and gaming, which afterwards he seemed very sensible of and sorrowful for; and as if it had been a good spirit that had guided him therein, he used a good method upon his conversion; for he declared he was ready to make restitution upon any man who would accuse him or whom he could accuse himself to have wronged: (to his honour I speak this; for I think public acknowledgments men make of the public evils they have done to be the most glorious trophies they can have assigned to them). When he was thus civilized, he joined himself to men of his own temper, who pretended unto transports and revelations.

Now not long after the Earl of Bedford and divers of the principal gentlemen whose habitations confined upon the Fens and who in the heat of summer saw vast quantities of lands, which the fresh waters overflowed in the winter, lie dry and green or drainable; whether it was public spirit or private advantage which led them thereunto, a stranger cannot determine: they make propositions unto the King to issue out commissions of Sewers to drain these lands, and offer a proportion freely to be given to the Crown for its countenance and authority therein. And as all these great and public works must necessarily concern multitudes of persons, who will never think they have exact justice done to them for that small pretence of right they have unto some commons, so the Commissioners, let them do what they can, could never satisfy such a body of men. And now the King is declared the principal undertaker for the draining; and by this time the vulgar are grown clamorous against the first popular Lords and undertakers who have joined with the King in the second undertaking, tho' they had much better provision with them than their interest was ever before: and the Commissioners must by the multitudes and clamours be withstood; and as the head of this faction, Mr Cromwell in the year 1638 at Huntingdon appears; which made his activity so well known unto his friend and kinsman, Mr Hampden, that in this parliament have a character of Cromwell being an active person and one that would sit well at the mark; and thus he is early joined unto the most busy contrivens of the new intended changes.

One thing more I have to observe concerning his temper, that whilst I was about Huntingdon, visiting old Sir Oliver Cromwell, his uncle and godfather, at his house at Ramsey, he told me this

story of his successful nephew and godson: that he visited him
with a strong party of horse and that he had asked him for his
blessing, and that the few hours he was there he would not keep on
his hat in his presence; but at the same time he not only disarmed
but plundered him: for he took away all his plate.

JOHN LILBURNE: "THE MAN THAT GOD HATH HONOURED" (1647) [2]

> *John Lilburne, leader of the radical group known as the
> Levellers, who in his younger days had been befriended by
> Cromwell, attacked all existing authorities at the end of the
> first civil war, including the leaders of the victorious Parlia-
> ment and army. In 1647, he was in prison in the Tower of
> London, having been put there by order of the House of
> Lords for libeling one of its members. While he was there
> he wrote to Cromwell a number of letters that later were
> included in a pamphlet entitled* Jonah's Cry out of the
> Whale's Belly. *The following is an extract from a letter dated
> March 25, 1647, and addressed to "The Man that God Hath
> Honoured and will further Honour if he continue Honouring
> Him, Lieu.-General Cromwell at his house in Drury Lane near
> the Red Lion." Its interest lies in its showing in a backhanded
> way Cromwell's immense popularity in the army. The House
> of Commons had voted £2,500 a year as a reward for his
> services as a commander in the civil wars. Lilburne implies
> that this reward was intended to make him disloyal to his
> own soldiers, which of course was not the case.*

It is the saying of a wise man that he "that rewardeth evil
for good, evil shall never depart from his house," the justness of
which divine sentence, engraven in nature, hath even engaged moral
heathen to a grateful acknowledgment of favours received and hath
been a sufficient obligation conscientiously to try them, to acts of
retribution to those from whom they have received them and therefore not only below a Christian but a very moral heathen and
pagan should I judge myself if I should be forgetful of your season-

[2] John Lilburne, *Jonah's Cry out of the Whale's Belly* (1647), pp. 1–4.

able favours, much more if I should return contrary effects unto you which, with all thankfulness, I must allow took compassion of me in my bonds and chains even more when I was at death's door in anno 1640, and setting me free from the long and dreary tyranny of the bishops and Star Chamber, even at that time when I was almost spent; which to me is as large an obligation that I think while I live it will be engraven upon my heart as with the point of a diamond, many particular respects, first then I must ingeniously confess I have cause to take notice of from you; and one large one of late since I came into present captivity which was for that large token you sent me, for which now in writing I return my thanks.

Sir, I dare not now by way of boasting take upon me to enumerate my hazardous activities which hath flowed from the truth of my affections to you in doing you real and faithful service, in maintaining the honour of your person, and your just interest which was all the retribution that I in my poor condition could answer all your kindnesses with. . . . God hath honoured you sufficiently for it, not only in giving you extraordinary large room in the affections of thousands, and tens of thousands of His chosen ones, but in hanging upon your back the glory of all their achievements, by means of which you have been made mighty and great, formidable and dreadful in the eyes of the great ones of the world; and truly myself and all of my mind that I could speak with, have looked upon you as the most single-hearted great man in England, untainted and unbiased with ends of your own. But, dear sir, give him leave that presumeth to say and that without flattery he honoureth you as he doth his own life and being. . . . O dear Cromwell, the Lord open thy eyes, and make thy heart sensible of those snares that are laid for thee in that vote of the House of Commons of two thousand five hundred pounds per annum.

And Deut. 16, 19 God saith expressly; "Thou shalt not wrest judgment, thou shalt not respect persons, neither take a gift: for a gift doth bind the eyes of the wise and pervert the words of the righteous." . . .

So I say to thee, thou great man Cromwell: Think not of thyself, that thou shalt escape into the parliament house, me than all the rest of the lambs, poor despised redeemed ones, and therefore o Cromwell, if thou altogether holdest thy peace (or stoppest or underminest as thou dost, ours and the Army's petitions) at this time then shall enlargement and deliverance arise to us poor afflicted ones (that have hitherto doted too much upon thee, o Cromwell) from another place than from you silken Independents, the broken reeds of Egypt in the House and Army) but thou and thy Father's house shall be destroyed: but who knoweth whether thou art come out of thy sickness, and to such a height in the kingdom, for such a time as this?

And therefore if thou wilt pluck up thy resolutions, like a man that will persevere to be a man for God, and go on, bravely in the fear and name of God and say with Esther, if I perish, I perish; but if thou would not, know that here before God I arraign thee at His dreadful bar, and there accuse thee of delusions and fair words, deceitfully for betraying us, our wives and children into the Haman-like tyrannous clutches of Hollis and Stapleton [Presbyterian leaders] (both now impeached) and the rest of that bloody and devouring faction that hath designed us to utter ruin and destruction, and this land and kingdom to vassalage and slavery, against which we are sufficiently able to persevere ourselves if it were not for thee, o Cromwell: thou art led by the nose by two unworthy covetous earthworms, Vane and St John (I mean young Sir Henry Vane and Solicitor St John) whose baseness I sufficiently anatomized unto thee in thy bed over a year ago in Colonel Mountagu's house in the Pears, as thou canst very well remember, and which I am resolved to the purpose shortly to print.

O Cromwell, I am informed this day by an officer out of the army, and by another knowing man yesterday that came a purpose to me out of the army, that you and your agents are likely to dash in pieces the hopes of our outward preservation, their petition to the House, and will not suffer them to petition till they have laid down their arms, because, forsooth, you have engaged to the House they shall lay down their arms whenever you shall command them; although I say no credit can be given to the House's oaths and engagements, to make good what they have promised. And if this be true, as I am too much afraid it is, then I say: Accursed be the day that ever you had that influence amongst them; and accursed be the day that ever the House of Commons bribed you with a vote of £2500 per annum to betray and destroy us. . . .

SIR LEWIS DYVE: CROMWELL AND LILBURNE (1647)[3]

As is made clear in the previous extract, John Lilburne thought in 1647 that Cromwell had been bribed by the House of Commons to suppress the grievances of the rank and file of the Parliamentary army and to prevent their petitioning for justice. In fact, however, Cromwell led his cavalry into London that very summer and brought pressure to bear upon Parliament to come to a settlement both with the army and with the King. Lilburne nevertheless insisted that Cromwell was now concerned only with his own personal advancement, while allowing true patriots like Lilburne himself to languish in prison. He also accused Cromwell of fawning upon the King. Cromwell, who naturally was anxious to prevent mutiny or anarchy in the army as a result of the dissemination of political propaganda by Lilburne and his friends, visited him in the Tower of London on September 6 with a view to pacifying him. Lilburne described this visit to his fellow prisoner, a Royalist named Sir Lewis Dyve, who sent his account on to Charles I.

In the evening after Cromwell's departure from hence, Lilburne made me a long relation of what passed between them, the most essential parts whereof I shall, according to the best of my memory, represent unto Your Majesty with as much brevity as I can, omitting nothing which I conceive material. After the first ceremonies of civility which (Lilburne said) were performed with great expression of kindness on Cromwell's behalf, they withdrew from the Lieutenant of the Tower and Cromwell, beginning to break the discourse, asked how it came to pass that he had fallen out with his best friends and was become so great an enemy to Parliament, advising him to patience and moderation, and not to

[3] "The Tower of London Letter-Book of Sir Lewis Dyve," 1646–47, ed. H. G. Tibbutt, *The Publications of the Bedfordshire Historical Record Society*, Vol. XXXVIII (1957), p. 85 ff.

speak with so much bitterness of the Parliament, but rather to suspend his judgment for a while and he should see the Parliament would speedily proceed to do those things which would render the kingdom happy and, [he] doubted not, much to his satisfaction.

And then pausing, gave Mr Lilburne leave to reply, who said that he neither had, nor ever would, fall out with his friends, but he saw with much grief of heart that those who he esteemed for his friends had fallen off both from him and [from] their first principles, which had engaged him in their service, whom he had served with all fidelity whilst he conceived their intentions to be just and honest and that in recompence thereof that they had cast him into prison where, contrary to all justice, they suffered him to remain to the utter undoing of himself, his wife, and children, when as he desireth no other favour but to be brought to a fair and legal trial, to be acquitted or condemned according to the merits of his cause, which he had long and earnestly solicited without effect, and therefore he was not to be blamed if he spake of the Parliament according to what he found to be their constant practice, not only to him in his own particular but unto all persons whatsoever that had anything to do with them, telling him withal that the greatest crimes they had objected against your Majesty's government was in comparison of the best of their actions, both glorious and righteous.

Cromwell replied that your Majesty's reign was a habit of oppression and tyranny, but that those things wherein the Parliament might seem to have swerved from the right rules of justice were rather by way of accident and necessity, which he should see speedily reformed as soon as those necessities were removed, and that in the meantime patience would best become prudent men until they had secured their own preservation.

Lilburne told him that the likeliest and best way whereby to preserve themselves would be impartially to do right and equally to administer justice towards all men and effectually to proceed to the settlement of the peace of the kingdom according to their own declarations, both in reference to your Majesty and the subjects' liberties, which they had so long delayed, since the power was absolutely in their own hands, as had not without cause drawn great jealousies upon themselves, and that the whole kingdom would shortly look upon the great men, both of the Parliament and the Army, as the only obstructors to the peace and happiness of the Kingdom and the contrivers of some new tyrannical government to be erected whereby to enslave the people to their own wills and pleasures.

Cromwell told him that fears were vain and that he believed they were the infusions of some subtle Cavaliers with whom he conversed, of whom he wished him to beware that they made him not as bad as themselves, of whom he would yet have a charitable opinion, though he saw him much corrupted to his first and best principles.

Lilburne said that therein he must mistook him, for that he had not vanished at all from his first principles, and that he was the self-same man as when he had the honour first to be known to him, detesting tyranny as well now as ever, from what hand soever it came, which he would to the uttermost of his power always endeavour to oppose in those that should exercise it against him in so high a degree as the Parliament had done, and that, in plain English, he would by all the ways he could possibly invent labour to destroy them, as he had formerly done the bishops, rather than that they should destroy him, his wife, and children by keeping him longer in prison.

Whereupon Cromwell asked him in case they should set him at liberty whether he would then be quiet. He said "no" unless he might withal have satisfaction for his losses, wrongs, and injuries, sustained by them. Cromwell told him that should be done if he would have patience, and in the meantime an honourable employment should be given him in the army until the other might with conveniency be effected according to his own desire.

Lilburne gave him thanks for the expression of his favour towards him, but said withal that as the case now stood, and according to those principles by which he perceived they now steered their course, he would not be engaged either in the parliament's or the army's service for all the gold in the world; but if he would be a means to procure his liberty upon those terms, he desired it, he would esteem himself highly obliged to him, and that when he should be satisfied with the justice of their ways, so as with a good conscience he might serve them, he would then accept thereof and perform it as faithfully as ever.

"Well," said Cromwell, "though you have given me little encouragement, yet such is the affection I bear you, as you shall see I will not be wanting in my best endeavours to procure your liberty of the Parliament, whereof I hope you shall find the effects in a very short time." . . .

> *Cromwell was as good as his word and by his intervention in Parliament, Lilburne shortly afterwards was released on bail. But Lilburne was an impossible man to deal with; he next accused Cromwell, quite unjustly, of intriguing with the Royalists, whereas this was in fact what he was engaged in doing himself.*[4]

EDMUND LUDLOW: A GOVERNMENT BASED ON ORDER NOT CONSENT (1650)[5]

> *Lieutenant-General Ludlow, who for a time was acting commander-in-chief of the English Parliamentary army in Ireland, was a keen republican and a consistent and bitter critic of Cromwell from the time when the latter expelled the remnant, or Rump, of the Long Parliament in 1653. He had several interviews with Cromwell, who eventually had him arrested. The first interview took place in 1650, after Cromwell's return from his Irish campaign.*

As I sat in the House [of Commons] near General Cromwell, he told me, having observed an alteration in my looks and carriage towards him, he apprehended that I had entertained some suspicions of him; and that being persuaded of the tendency of the designs of us both to the advancement of the public service, he desired that a meeting might be appointed, wherein we might

---

[4] See Maurice Ashley, "Oliver Cromwell and the Levellers," *History Today*, XVII, No. 8 (August, 1967).

[5] Edmund Ludlow, *Memoirs*, ed. C. H. Firth (1894), I, 244–46.

with freedom discover the grounds of our mistakes and misapprehensions, and create a good understanding between us for the future . . .

I freely acknowledged my former dissatisfaction with him and the rest of the army, when they were in treaty with the King [in 1647], whom I looked upon as the only obstruction to the settlement of the nation; and with their actions at the rendezvous at Ware [November, 1647], where they shot a soldier to death, and imprisoned divers others upon the account of that treaty, which I conceived to have been done without authority, and for sinister ends; yet since they had manifested themselves convinced of those errors, and declared their adherence to the Commonwealth, tho' too partial a hand was carried both by the parliament and by themselves in the distribution of preferments and gratuities, and too much severity exercised against some who had formerly been their friends, and as I hoped would be so still, with other things that I could not entirely approve, I was contented patiently to wait for the accomplishment of those good things which I expected, till they had overcome the difficulties they now laboured under, and suppressed their enemies that appeared both at home and abroad against them; hoping that then their principles and interest would lead them to do what was most agreeable to the constitution of a Commonwealth, and the good of mankind.

He owned my dissatisfaction with the army whilst they were in treaty with the King to be founded upon good reasons, and excused the execution done upon the soldier at the rendezvous as absolutely necessary to keep things from falling into confusion, which must have ensued upon that division, if it had not been timely prevented. He professed to desire nothing more than the government of the nation might be settled in a free and equal Commonwealth, acknowledging that there was no other probable means to keep out the old family and government from returning upon us; declaring that he looked upon the design of the Lord in this day to be the freeing of His people from every burden, and that He was now accomplishing what was prophesied in the 110th Psalm; from the consideration of which he was often encouraged to attend the effecting those ends, spending at least an hour in the exposition of that Psalm, adding to this that it was his intention to contribute the ut-

most of his endeavours to make a thorough reformation of the
clergy and law: but, he said, "the sons of Zeruiah are yet too strong
for us"; and we cannot mention the reformation of the law, but they
presently cry out we design to destroy property: whereas the law, as
it is now constituted, serves only to maintain the lawyers, and to
encourage the rich to oppress the poor; affirming that Mr Coke,
then Justice in Ireland, by proceeding in a summary and expedi-
tious way, determined more causes in a week than Westminster Hall
in a year; saying farther, that Ireland was a clean paper in that
particular, and capable of being governed by such laws as should
be found most agreeable to justice; which may be so impartially
administered as to be a good precedent to England itself . . .

[Ludlow eventually was arrested after his return from Ireland,
where he had refused to recognize the Protectorate. He was brought
before Cromwell in the summer of 1656.]

I drew near to the Council table where Cromwell charged me
with dispersing treasonable books in Ireland and with endeavouring to render the officers of the army disaffected by discoursing to
them concerning new models of government. I acknowledged that
I had caused some papers to be dispersed in Ireland, but denied
that they justly could be called treasonable. And though I knew
it was a crime to debate of the several forms of government, yet
that I had not done any thing of that nature lately to the best of
my remembrance. He then said that he was not ignorant of the
many plots that were on foot to disturb the present power and
that he thought it his duty to secure such as he suspected. To this
I replied that there were two duties required by God of the magistrate i.e. that he be a terror to those that do evil and a praise to
such as do well; and whether my actions were good or bad, I was
ready to submit to a legal trial: that I was ignorant of any other
way to secure the magistrate from being afraid of the people, or
the people from the dread of the magistrate, unless both will do
that which is just and good.

"You do well," said he, "to reflect on our fears; yet I would
have you know that what I do proceeds not from any motive of
fear but from a timely prudence to foresee and prevent danger; that
had I done as I should, I ought to have secured you immediately

upon your coming into England or at least when you desired to be freed from the engagement you had given after your arrival; and therefore I now require you to give assurance not to act against the Government." I desired to be excused in that particular, reminding him of the reasons I had formerly given him for my refusal, adding that I was in his power, and that he might use me as he thought fit. "Pray then," said he, "what is it that you would have? May not every man be as good as he will? What can you desire more than you have?" "It were easy," said I, "to tell what we would have." "What is that, I pray," said he. "That which we fought for," said I, "that the nation might be governed by its own consent." "I am," said he, "as much for government by consent as any man; but where shall we find that consent? Amongst the Prelatical, Presbyterian, Independent, Anabaptist, or Levelling Parties?" I answered; "Amongst those of all sorts who had acted with fidelity and affection to the public."

Then he fell into the commendation of his own government, boasting of the protection and quiet which the people enjoyed under it, saying that he was resolved to keep the nation from being imbrued in blood. I said that I was of the opinion too much blood had already been shed, unless there were a better account of it. "You do well," said he, "to charge us with the guilt of blood; but we think there is a good return for what hath been shed; and we understand what clandestine correspondences are carrying on at this time between the Spaniard and those of your party, who make use of your name, and affirm that you will own them and assist them." "I know not," said I, "what you mean by my party, and can truly say that if any men have entered into an engagement with Spain, they had no advice from me so to do and that if they will use my name, I cannot help it." Then in a softer way he told that he desired not to put any more hardships on me than on himself; that he had always been ready to do me all the good offices that lay in his power and that he aimed at nothing by this proceeding but the public quiet and security. "Truly, sir," said I, "I know not why you should be an enemy to me who have been faithful to you in all your difficulties." "I understand not," said he, "what you mean by my difficulties. I am sure they were not so properly mine as those of the public; for in respect of my outward condition I have not much improved it, as these gentlemen," pointing to his Council, "well know . . ."

BULSTRODE WHITELOCKE: "WHAT IF A MAN SHOULD TAKE UPON HIM TO BE A KING" (1652) [6]

Bulstrode Whitelocke was a member of the Council of State and, for a time, the English ambassador in Sweden during the Interregnum. His Memorials were published after the restoration of Charles II in 1682. My own view is that they were embroidered and are not altogether trustworthy, but they have been accepted by most of Cromwell's biographers. The following conversation is assigned by Whitelocke to 1652, that is, before the establishment of the Protectorate.

Cromwell: I can trust you with my life and the most secret matters relating to our business, and to that end I have now desired a little private discourse with you; and really, my lord, there is very great cause for us to consider the dangerous condition we are all in, and how to make good our station, to improve the mercies and successes which God hath given us, and not to be fooled out of them again, nor to be broken in pieces by our particular jarrings and animosities against one another, but to unite our counsels and hands and hearts, to make good what we have so dearly bought with so much hazard, blood, and treasure; and that the Lord having given us an entire conquest over our enemies, we should not now hazard all again by our private janglings, and bring those mischiefs upon ourselves which our enemies could never do.

Whitelocke: My lord, I look upon our present danger as greater than ever it was in the field, and (as your excellency truly observes) our proneness to destroy ourselves, when our enemies could not do it. It is no strange thing for a gallant army (as yours is) after full conquest of their enemies, to grow into factions and ambitious designs, and it is a wonder to me that they are not in high mutinies,

---

[6] Bulstrode Whitelocke, *Memorials of the English Affairs* (ed. 1853), IV, 469–72.

their spirits being active and few thinking their services to be duly rewarded, and the emulation of the officers breaking out daily more and more in this time of their vacancy from employment; besides the private soldiers, it may be feared, will in this time of their idleness grow into disorder, and it is your excellent conduct which, under God, hath kept them so long in discipline and free from mutinies.

Cromwell: I have used and shall use the utmost of my poor endeavours to keep them all in order and obedience.

Whitelocke: Your excellency hath done it hitherto even to admiration.

Cromwell: Truly God hath blessed me in it exceedingly, and I hope will do so still. Your lordship hath observed most truly the inclinations of the officers of the army to particular factions and to murmurings that they are not rewarded according to their deserts, that others who have adventured least have gained most, and they have neither profit nor preferment nor place in the government, which others hold who have undergone no hardships nor hazards for the Commonwealth; and herein they have too much of truth, yet their insolency is very great and their influence upon the private soldiers works them to the like discontents and murmurings.

Then as for the members of parliament, the army begins to have a strange distaste against them, and I wish there were not too much cause for it, and really their pride and ambition and self-seeking, engrossing all places of honour and profit to themselves and their friends, and their daily breaking forth into new and violent parties and factions; their delays of business and design to perpetuate themselves and to continue the power in their own hands; their meddling in private matters between party and party, contrary to the institution of parliaments; and their injustice and partiality in those matters and the scandalous lives of some of the chief of them; these things, my lord, do give too much ground for people to open their mouths against them and to dislike them.

Nor can they be kept within the bounds of justice and law or reason, they themselves being the supreme power of the nation, liable to no account to any nor to be controlled or regulated by any other power; there being none superior or coordinate with them. So that unless there be some authority and power so full and so high as to restrain and keep things in better order and that may be a check upon their exorbitances, it will be impossible in human reason to prevent our ruin.

Whitelocke: I confess the danger we are in by these extravagances and inordinate powers is more than I doubt is generally apprehended; yet as to that part of it which concerns the soldiery, your excellency's power and commission is sufficient already to restrain and keep them in their due obedience and, blessed be God, you have done it hitherto, and I doubt not by your wisdom you will be able still to do it.

As to the members of parliament, I confess the greatest difficulty there, your commission being from them and they being acknowledged the supreme power of the nation, subject to no controls nor allowing any appeal from them. I am sure your excellency will not look upon them as generally depraved, too many of them are much to blame in those things you have mentioned and many unfit things have passed among them; but I hope well of the major part of them when great matters come to a decision.

Cromwell: My lord, there is little hope of a good settlement to be made by them, really there is not; but a great deal of fear that they will destroy again what the Lord hath done graciously for them and us; we all forget God, and God will forget us and give us up to confusion: and these men will help it on, if they be suffered to proceed in their ways; some course must be thought on to curb and restrain them or we shall be ruined by them.

Whitelocke: We ourselves have acknowledged them the supreme power and taken our commissions and authority in the highest concernments from them, and how to restrain and curb them after this it will be hard to find out a way for it.

Cromwell: What if a man should take upon him to be a king?

Whitelocke: I think that remedy would be worse than the disease.

Cromwell: Why do you think so?

Whitelocke: As to your own person, the title of king would be of no advantage because you have the full kingly power in you already concerning the militia, as you are General. As to the nomination of civil officers, those whom you think fittest are seldom refused; and although you have no negative vote in the passing of laws, yet what you dislike will not easily be carried, and the taxes are already settled and in your power to dispose the money raised. And as to foreign affairs, though the ceremonial application be made to the parliament, yet the expectation of good or bad success in it is from your excellency, and particular solicitations of foreign ministers are made to you only.

So that I apprehend indeed less envy and danger and pomp but no less power and real opportunities of doing good in your being General than would be if you had assumed the title of King.

Cromwell: I have heard some of your profession observe that he who is actually king, whether by election or descent, yet being once king, all acts done by him as king are lawful and justifiable as by any king who hath the crown by inheritance from his forefathers; and that by an act of parliament in Henry VII's time it is safer for those who act under a king (be his title what it will) than for those who act under any other power.

And surely the power of a king is so great and high and so universally understood and reverenced by the people of this nation that the title of it might not only indemnify in a great measure those that act under it, but likewise be of great use and advantage in such times as these, to curb the insolences and extravagances of those whom the present powers cannot control or at least are the persons themselves who are thus insolent. . . .

JOHN ROGERS: SUFFERING FOR THE FAITH [7]

John Rogers, like Christopher Feake—both are mentioned below—was a preacher who belonged to the sect known as the Fifth Monarchy Men. They believed in the imminent coming of Jesus Christ to reign upon earth and, pending his coming, they disapproved of all earthly rulers. Like the Fighting

[7] Edward Rogers, *Some Account of the Life and Opinions of a Fifth Monarchy-Man* (1867), pp. 190–97.

*Quakers, they constantly disturbed the public peace by their
extreme behavior, which included breaking up services held
in churches by other Christians. As disturbers of the peace,
Rogers and Feake were arrested and imprisoned after they
refused to give guarantees of good behavior. They were re-
leased later, but subsequently had to be arrested again.
Cromwell preferred that they should not be charged in courts
of law, lest they be condemned to death for blasphemy or
mutilated as the Quaker James Naylor was to be in December,
1656, by order of the House of Commons acting (improperly)
as a court. In February, 1655, a group of Fifth Monarchy Men
interviewed Cromwell in order to try to persuade him to
release Rogers and Feake. Rogers himself was present at this
interview, which was recounted from the Fifth Monarchy
Men's point of view in a contemporary pamphlet entitled*
The Faithfull Narrative. *The following is an extract purport-
ing to report the dialogue between Cromwell and Rogers.
If it is compared with Cromwell's interviews with Lilburne
(above p. 84) and with Fox (below p. 117), it will be seen how
Cromwell was prepared to tolerate liberty of conscience, provided the individuals who enjoyed it were willing to respect
law and order.*

Cromwell: I promised to send for you, for some of your friends
came and spoke sharply to me, as if I had apostated from the cause
of Christ and [was] persecuting godly ministers, namely Mr Rogers
and Mr Feake; [you] spake other things that were sharp enough.
You might have had patience in your words. Now you have liberty
to speak to those things, but do not abuse your liberty. You told
me Mr Rogers suffered as a railer, a seducer, and a busybody in
other men's matters and a stirrer up of sedition, which rulers, led
by just principles, might suppress. I told you Mr Rogers suffered
justly, and not for the testimony of Jesus Christ; and indeed, in
some degree, it is blasphemy to call suffering for evil-doing suffering for the Gospel; and if he suffers for railing and despising those
that God hath set over him, to say that his suffering is for the
Gospel, is making Christ the patron of such things; but if it were
suffering for the Gospel, something might have been said, yet not
so much as saying uncharitably he suffered for evil-doing; so if we

show you you suffer for transgression, then you abuse that Scripture, which I have often thought on, that it is "to make a man an offender for a word." I wish it were better understood in the plainness of the spirit, for (to interpret that Scripture) it was the evil of those times, which was to lie in wait for words on purpose to catch at words without actions and words are conjugal with actions, for actions and words are as sharp as swords, and such things I charge you with, and you suffer not for the testimony of Christ. I speak— God is my witness—I know it, that no man in England does suffer for the testimony of Jesus. Nay, do not lift up your hands and your eyes, for there is no man in England which suffers so. There are those that are far better than Mr Rogers, though comparisons are not good, and not near his principles, yet if they should suffer [it would be] for the testimony of Jesus. But there is such liberty; I wish it not abused, that no man in England suffereth for Christ; and it is not your fancy. You must bring strong words to acquaint me of your sharp expressions.

Rogers: Do you expect me to answer? I will premise this before I speak further: I have been twenty-seven weeks a prisoner (my brother Feake above a year) and there hath been no charge against me. But now I have been brought before you—as a prisoner or as a freeman; as a Christian to a Christian, with equal freedom that others have, or a slave?

Cromwell: A prisoner is a freeman, as Christ hath made you free, and so you are a freeman. . . . I told you he [Rogers] suffered as an evil-doer, as a railer, as a seducer.

Rogers: But your words are not proofs, my lord. But yet, seeing my way is more clear now, I shall say something more; there is no law of God nor yet of man that makes me such an offender but yours, which is worse than the Roman law and it is tyranny that makes a man a traitor for words.

Cromwell: Who calls you a traitor? I call you not. See, I believe you speak many things according to the Gospel, but you suffer for evil-doing.

Rogers: The Gospel of the Kingdom may occasionally be so accounted and judged; for Christ our Saviour saith: "I came not to send peace but the sword." The doctrine of Christ by the powers of the world hath ever been reputed sedition, railing, lying, and speaking evil of dignities.

Cromwell: I grieve you call this the Gospel; for everyone is ready to come and say this is the meaning of the Scripture but this wants the power of godliness, for Christ and His disciples will not speak evil of no man.

Rogers: Yea, they speak against sinners as sinners,which is no evil-speaking. But who made you the judge of the Scriptures my Lord? . . . It is true this present testimony for Christ's Kingly Interest hath two parts, viz. the positive and the privative; now for the last it is we suffer, and not for evil-doing.

Cromwell: Why, who will hinder your preaching the Gospel of Christ—yea His Personal Reign? Who will hinder? You speak of high notions, but you do not preach the Gospel to build up souls in Christ.

Rogers: I know, my lord, that you are a sophister. And so it seems [that] for a part of the truth we may preach, but not the whole [truth] not the Gospel of the Kingdom preached for a witness, as Matt. xxiv, to witness against the crying sins of men in power and out of power; for that seems to strike at your interest too much.

Cromwell: Why, what interest is mine?

Rogers: A worldly interest which God will destroy.

Cromwell: Ha!—and do you judge me?

Rogers: Yea, by the word of the Lord. . . . Besides I am called by the Holy Ghost, which hath appointed me to preach the Gospel, to judge sins.

Cromwell: And who will hinder you to preach the Gospel or to do so?—speak against sin as much as you will.

JOHN MILTON: "OUR CHIEF OF MEN" [8]

The first quotation is the ode that Milton composed in 1652 after Cromwell's return from his victories at Dunbar

[8] John Milton, *Poetic Works*, ed. Helen Darbyshire (1962), II, 153–54.

and Worcester, but before he became Lord Protector. The second is a prose extract from A Second Defence of the English People *written in May, 1654, in answer to an "anonymous libel."*

Cromwell, our chief of men, who through a cloud
    Not of war only, but detractions rude,
    Guided by faith and matchless fortitude,
To peace and truth thy glorious way hast ploughed,
And on the neck of crowned fortune proud
    Hast rear'd God's trophies, and His work pursued,
    When Darwen stream with blood of Scots imbrued,
And Dunbar field resounds thy praises loud,
And Worcester's laureate wreath: Yet much remains
    To conquer still; peace hath her victories
    No less renown'd than war: new foes arise
Threatening to bind our souls with secular chains:
    To help us to save free conscience from the paw
    Of hireling wolves, whose gospel is their maw.

"A BULWARK TO ALL GOOD MEN, A TERROR TO THE WICKED" [9]

Oliver Cromwell is sprung of renowned and illustrious stock. The name was celebrated in former times for good administration under the monarchy and became more glorious as soon as the orthodox religion was reformed, or rather established amongst us for the first time. He had grown up in the seclusion of his own home, until he reached an age mature and settled, and this too he passed as a private citizen, known for nothing so much as his devotion to the Puritan religion and his upright life. For an occasion of supreme importance he had nourished in his silent heart a faith dependent on God and a mighty spirit. When parliament was for the last time convened by the king, Cromwell was chosen by his town's electorate and won a seat. There he at once became known for his upright sentiments and steadfast counsels. When war broke out, he offered his services and was put in command of a squadron

[9] John Milton, *The Second Defence of the People of England* (1806), VI, 432–33.

of horse, but because of the concourse of good men who flocked to his standards from all sides, his force was greatly increased and he soon surpassed well-nigh the greatest generals both in the magnitude of his accomplishments and in the speed with which he achieved them. Nor was this remarkable, for he was a soldier well-versed in self-knowledge, and whatever enemy lay within—vain hopes, fears, desires—he had either previously destroyed within himself or had long since reduced to subjection. Commander first over himself, victor over himself, he had learned to achieve over himself the most effective triumph, and so, on the very first day that he took service against an external foe, he entered camp a veteran and past-master in all that concerned the soldier's life.

It is impossible for me within the confines of this discourse to describe with fitting dignity the capture of the many cities, to list the many battles, and indeed such great ones, in which he was never conquered nor put to flight, but traversed the entire realm of Britain with uninterrupted victory. Such deeds require the grand scope of true history, a second battlefield, so to speak, on which they may be recounted, and a space for narration equal to the deeds themselves. The following single proof of his rare and all-but-divine excellence suffices—that there flourished in him so great a power, whether of intellect and genius or of discipline (established according not merely to military standards, but rather according to the code of Christian virtue) that to his camp, as to the foremost school, not just of military science, but of religion and piety, he attracted from every side all men who were already good and brave, or else he had made them such, chiefly by his own example. Throughout the entire war, and sometimes even in the intervening periods of peace, amid the many shifts of opinion and circumstance, in spite of opposition, he kept them at their duty, and does so still, not by bribes and licentiousness typical of the military, but by his authority and their wages alone. No greater praise is won to be attributed to Cyrus or Epaminondas or any other pre-eminent general among the ancients.

And so no one has ever raised a large or better-disciplined army in a shorter space of time than did Cromwell, an army obedient to his command in all things, welcomed and cherished by their fellow citizens, formidable indeed to the enemy in the field, but wonderfully merciful to them once they had surrendered. On the estates and under the roofs of the enemy this army proved so mild and innocent of all offence that when the royalists considered the violence of their own soldiery, their drunkenness, impiety, and lust, they rejoiced in their altered lot and believed that Cromwell's men had come, not as enemies, but as guests, a bulwark to all good men, a terror to the wicked, and in fact an inspiration to all virtue and piety.

EDMUND LUDLOW: CROMWELL AND THE CROWN [10]

Edmund Ludlow was a vehement republican, and his story of Cromwell's reaction to the offer of the Crown by Parliament must be judged prejudiced. But on the whole, his account is pretty accurate, as we know because Cromwell's own speeches to the delegation that offered him the title of King have survived (see p. 74 above):

Many objections being made in the House [of Commons] against the Instrument of Government, Cromwell, who was vehemently desirous to be a king, began to think it altogether insignificant to that purpose, and that it would be more conducing to his design if a new form were drawn up and presented to the assembly for their approbation. Accordingly it was prepared by his creatures, and brought into the House by Mr Pack, an alderman of London, where it was without much difficulty read, and appeared to be a shoe fitted to the foot of a monarch, though at present a blank was left for the title of the single person, who with two Houses was to have the supreme legislative power. . . .

Yet for all this he [Cromwell] scrupled to take upon him the title of king, as a thing scandalous and of great hazard; though at the same time he vilified the former Instrument of Government to the last degree; and after having so highly magnified it when it was established, he compared it now to a rotten plank, on which if a man set his foot, it will break and leave him. The Assembly well understanding that the cause of his delays was either to be im-

[10] Edmund Ludlow, *Memoirs*, ed. C. H. Firth (1894), II, 21–28.

portuned to the thing or to get time to persuade the army to be of the same opinion with himself, appointed a committee of its own members to give him the reasons for accepting that title. Amongst others the Lord Broghill much pressed that passage brought by the apostle in the dispute concerning the abolition of the Jewish worship by the new and living way revealed in Jesus Christ illustrated by the wife that was put away, who might yet be retaken by her former husband, if she was not married to another; applying this similitude to the present occasion, as if there were no other way to keep out Charles Stewart, but by filling his place with another king. Mr Lenthall's argument was very parliamentary and rational, had it been rightly applied; for he pressed him to accept of it because it was proposed to him by the parliament, as he was pleased to call it, whom he said he ought not to deny. But he was now arrived to that height of vanity, that though the design of this argument was only to persuade him to accept that which he desired above all things in the world, yet conceiving it below his grandeur to acknowledge such a prerogative in the parliament alone, he expressed his dislike of it. And though he owned that the reasons they had offered had much weight in them and that he was convinced there was no evil in the thing, yet he could not think it expedient to accept their offer, because he found that many of the good people of the nation were dissatisfied with it.

With this answer he dismissed them for the present and appointed them to attend him again. In the meantime he endeavoured by all possible means to prevail with the officers of the army to approve his design, and knowing that Lieutenant-General Fleetwood and Col. Desborough were particularly averse to it, he invited himself to dine personally with the Colonel and carried the Lieutenant-General with him, where he began to droll with them about monarchy, and speaking slightly of it, said it was but a feather in a man's cap, and therefore wondered that men would not please the children, and permit them to enjoy their rattle. But he received from them, as Col. Desborough since told me, such an answer as was not at all suitable to his expectations or desires. For they assured him that there was more in this matter than they perceived; that those who put him upon it were no enemies to Charles

Stewart; and that if he accepted of it, he would infallibly draw ruin upon himself and his friends.

Having thus sounded their inclinations, that he might conclude in the manner he had begun, he told them they were a couple of scrupulous fellows, and so departed. The next day he sent a message to the House to require their attendance in the Painted Chamber the next morning, designing, as all men believed, there to declare his acceptance of the Crown. But in the meantime meeting with Col. Desborough in the great walk of the park and acquainting him with his resolution, the Colonel made answer that he then gave the cause and Cromwell's family also for lost; adding that although he was resolved never to act against him, yet he would not act for him after that time. So after some other discourse upon the same subject, Desborough went home, and there found Colonel Pride, whom Cromwell had knighted with a faggotstick; and having imparted to him the design of Cromwell to accept the Crown, Pride answered: "he shall not." "Why," said the Colonel, "how wilt thou hinder it?" To which Pride replied: "Get me a petition drawn, and I will prevent it." Whereupon they both went to Dr Owen, and having acquainted him with what happened, they persuaded him to draw a petition according to their desires.

Whilst this was doing, Cromwell, having reflected upon his discourse with Col. Desborough, and being informed that Lambert and divers other officers were dissatisfied with his design, sent a message to put off the meeting in the Painted Chamber, and to desire that the House would send a committee to confer with him about the great business that was then depending; intending thereby to gain time in which he might be fitting the officers for his design. But the House being risen before his message arrived, and so out of a capacity to appoint any to come to him, the old committee that had been formerly appointed to that end thought fit by virtue of their general instructions to wait on him to know his pleasure. Accordingly they came to Whitehall, where they attended about two hours, and then a Barbary horse being brought into the garden for him to see gave him occasion to pass through the room where the committee was attending. As he was passing by without taking the least notice of them, one of the messengers put him in mind that they had attended him very long; which he slightly excusing, told them that he thought the House being risen before his message came to them, had not empowered any persons to come to him. It was answered that they came to him upon the general instructions which they had formerly received from the House; upon which he told them he would send to them some other time.

The next morning the House being in great expectation of a message to appoint the time and place for the acceptance of what they had prepared, some officers of the army coming to the parliament doors, sent in a message to Colonel Desborough to acquaint him that they had a petition which they desired him to present to the House. But he, knowing the contents of it, and conceiving it unfit for him to take public notice of it before it was presented, acquainted the House that certain officers of the army had a petition to present to them. Which having done, and everyone supposing that the desires of the officers were conformable to their own, Cromwell's party concluding that no part of the army durst appear for the crossing his design, it was generally agreed that they should be called in and have leave to present it with their own hands. Lieutenant-Colonel Mason was chosen by the rest of the officers to deliver the petition, which when he had done and the officers withdrawn, it was read.

The contents of it were to this purpose: "That they had hazarded their lives against the monarchy, and were still ready so to do in defence of the liberties of the nation; that having observed in some men great endeavours to bring the nation under the old servitude by pressing their General to take upon him the title and government of a king, in order to destroy him and weaken the hands of those who were faithful to the public, they therefore humbly desired that they would discountenance all such persons and endeavours, and continue steadfast to the old cause, for the preservation of which they for their parts were most ready to lay down their lives." This petition was subscribed by two colonels, seven lieutenant-colonels, eight majors, and sixteen captains, who with such officers in the House as were of the same opinion, made up the majority of those relating to that part of the army which were then quartered about the town. It's difficult to determine whether the

House or Cromwell was more surprised at this unexpected address; but certainly both were infinitely disturbed by it.

As soon as the notice of it was brought to Cromwell, he sent for Lieutenant-General Fleetwood and told him that he wondered that he would suffer such a petition to proceed so far, which he might have hindered, since he knew it to be his resolution not to accept the Crown without the consent of the army; and therefore desired him to hasten to the House and to put them off from doing anything farther therein. The Lieutenant-General immediately went thither, and told them that the petition ought not to be debated, much less to be answered at this time, the contents of it being to desire them not to press the Protector to be King, whereas the present business was to receive his answer to what had been formerly offered to him, and therefore desired that the debate of it might be put off till they had received his answer. To this the House having consented, they received a message from Cromwell that, instead of meeting him in the Painted Chamber, which was the place where he used to give his consent, they would meet him in the Banqueting House: so the members came to Whitehall, and Cromwell with great ostentation of his self-denial refused the title of king.

RICHARD BAXTER: A DISSIMULATOR [11]

Richard Baxter was a leading Presbyterian minister who refused a chaplaincy in one of Cromwell's regiments and also refused a bishopric after the restoration of Charles II. He was a prolific writer.

If after so many others I may speak my opinion of him [Cromwell], I think that, having been a prodigal in his youth, and afterwards changed to a zealous religiousness, he meant honestly in the main course of his life till prosperity and success corrupted him; that, at his first entrance into the wars, being but a captain of horse, he had a special care to get religious men into his troop:

[11] *Reliquiae Baxterianae* (1696), pp. 98–100.

these men were of greater understanding than common soldiers, and therefore were more apprehensive of the importance and consequence of the war; and making not money, but that which they took for the public felicity to be their end, they were the more engaged to be valiant: for he that maketh money his end doth esteem his life above his pay, and therefore is like enough to save it by flight when danger comes if he possibly can. . . .

These things it's probable Cromwell understood; and that none should be such engaged, valiant men as the religious. But yet I conjecture that at his first choosing such men into his troop, it was the very esteem and love of religiousness that principally moved him; and the avoiding of those disorders, mutinies, plunderings and grievances of the country which debased men in armies are commonly guilty of. By this means he indeed sped better than he expected. Aires, Desborough, Berry, Evanson and the rest of that troop did prove so valiant that, as far as I could learn, they never once ran away before an enemy. Hereupon he got a commission to take some of the Associated Counties when he brought this troop into a double regiment of fourteen full troops; and all these as full of religious men as he could get: these, having more than ordinary wit and resolution, had more than ordinary success: first in Lincolnshire and afterward in the Earl of Manchester's army at York fight: with their successes the hearts both of captain and soldiers secretly rise in pride and expectation: and the familiarity of many honest erroneous men (Anabaptists, Antinomians, etc.) withal began quickly to corrupt their judgments.

Hereupon Cromwell's general religious zeal giveth way to the power of that ambition which still increaseth as his successes do increase: both piety and ambition concurred in his countenancing of all that he thought godly: and charity as men; and ambition secretly telleth him what use he might make of them. He meaneth well in all this at the beginning and thinketh he doth all for the safety of the godly and the public good, but not without an eye for himself.

When successes had broken down all considerable opposition he was then in the face of his strongest temptations which conquered him when he had conquered others. . . .

Having thus forced his conscience to justify all his cause (the cutting off the King, the setting up himself and his adherents, the pulling down the Parliament and the Scots) he thinketh that the end being good and necessary, the necessary means cannot be bad. And accordingly he giveth his interest and cause leave to tell him how far sects shall be tolerated and commended and how far not; and how far the ministry shall be owned and how far not; yea, and how far professions, promises and vows shall be kept or broken; and thereupon the Covenant he could not away with; nor the ministers further than they yielded to his ends or did not openly resist them.

He seemed exceeding open-hearted by a familiar rustic affected carriage (especially to his soldiers in sporting with them): but he thought secrecy a virtue and dissimulation no vice and simulation, that is, in plain English, a lie or perfidiousness to be a tolerable fault in a case of necessity: being of the same opinion with Lord Bacon, who was not so precise as learned, that the best composition and temperature is to have openness in fame and opinion, secrecy in habit, dissimulation in seasonable use, and a power to feign if there be no remedy—Essay, 6, page 31. Therefore he kept fair with all, saving his open and irreconcilable enemies. He carried it with such dissimulation that Anabaptists, Independents, and Antinomians did all think he was one of them. But he never endeavoured to persuade the Presbyterians that he was one of them, but only that he would do them justice and preserve them, and that he honoured their worth and piety, for he knew they were not so easily deceived. . . .

ANONYMOUS: "BLOODTHIRSTY TYRANT" (1657?) [12]

The following is a contemporary attack on Cromwell as a dictator. It was contained in an anonymous letter sent to Cromwell's son-in-law, Lieutenant-General Charles Fleetwood, apparently in 1657. This extract is printed because it was written during the Protectorate and is therefore preferred to Royalist lucubrations written after Cromwell was dead.

[12] "Well-wisher-in-chief to Lieutenant-General Fleetwood," *Thurloe State Papers,* VII, 204–5.

Now, my lord, 'tis not to be denied that your father [in-law] (with his courtiers) hath by force invaded the whole right and property of the people in their persons and estates. He assumed to himself (as he declared in his speech in parliament) an absolute arbitrary, unlimited power over their persons and estates; though he should have remembered that supreme empire is bounded by the rules of God, of nature, and nations. He hath spoiled the people of all rights in their persons, taking to himself an absolute power of life and death, imposing upon them his ordinances under capital punishment, and also taking what part of their estates he pleaseth, and filling gaols with their persons at his will, against his last oath, without crime or charge. Thus considering the blood he hath shed, the cause he hath pretended and the oaths wherewith he hath obliged himself, hath he not declared by his works (which are much clearer than printed declarations) that he esteems the sacred laws of God and nature (which forbid the invasion of other men's rights) to be no more than spider's webs that can only bind the feeble flies; and that whosover can by force nay (without dread of divine law) drink the blood of thousands and tens of thousands to compass the ends of greatness and dominion; and that oaths bind only those who cannot break them with impunity from men? In fine, hath not his works inclined the world to say . . . that your preaching, praying and precise sectaries, your godly men pretend no principles of justice, only for base and by-ends; and that there is no godliness but hypocrisy or indeed that there is no such just holy God as is pretended?

My lord, your father's works would not so plainly preach to the world these doctrines of devils nor cause the name of God to be so much blasphemed, if he did not avow the power he useth and all he does to be lawful, still professing godliness; whereas the whole world, Christian and pagan (that believe there is right and justice) have always agreed that the laws of nature have forbidden that any man should facilely assume the disposal of the lives, members and liberties of others in regard these were and would have remained proper to every man, if civil dominion and propriety of possessions had not been introduced; and likewise Greeks and Barbarians have always agreed the performance of promises and oaths (where the matter of them is lawful) to be of natural and divine right, and the obligation of them most sacred, the greatest assurance amongst men and the very bands and ligaments which hold together and preserve humane society.

But if all be excused with the pretence that the providences of God hath led him by steps to do all that he hath done, that plea will be found upon true inquiry to pollute the name of God more; for the Holy God directs and leads his people only into the path of righteousness, that is unto such actions as agree with His natural and voluntary divine laws: "He that doeth not righteousness is not of God."

EDMUND WALLER: "OUR DYING HERO" [18]

Edmund Waller, one of the outstanding poets of the seventeenth century, wrote an ode on Cromwell's death in 1658. He also wrote an ode upon His Majesty's happy return in 1660. The poem is entitled "Upon the late storm, and of the death of His Highness ensuing the same." It is sometimes said that Cromwell died during a storm. But it seems that the storms began on August 30, 1658; and ceased before Cromwell died, about three o'clock on September 3.

We must resign! Heaven his great soul does claim
In storms, as loud as his immortal fame;
His dying groans, his last breath, shakes our isle,
And trees uncut fall for his funeral pile;
About his palace their broad roots are tossed
Into the air.—So Romulus was lost.
New Rome in such a tempest missed her king,
And from obeying fell to worshipping.
On Oeta's top thus Hercules lay dead,
With ruined oaks and pines about him spread.
Those his last fury from the mountain rent:
Our dying hero from the continent
Ravished whole towns; and forts from Spaniards reft,
As his last legacy to Britain left.
The ocean, which so long our hopes confined,
Could give no limits to his vaster mind;

[18] Edmund Waller, *Poems*, ed. G. Thorn Drury (1893), pp. 162–63.

Our bounds' enlargement was his latest toil,
Nor hath he left us prisoners to our isle;
Under the tropic is our language spoke,
And part of Flanders hath received our yoke.
From civil broils he did us disengage,
Found nobler objects for our martial rage;
And, with wise conduct, to his country showed
Their ancient way of conquering abroad.
Ungrateful then! if we no tears allow
To him, that gave us peace and empire too.
Princes, that feared him, grieve, concerned to see
No pitch of glory from the grave us free.
Nature herself took notice of his death,
And, sighing, swelled the sea with such a breath,
That, to remotest shores her billows rolled,
The approaching fate of her great ruler told.

ANDREW MARVELL: "HE FIRST PUT ARMS INTO RELIGION'S HAND" [14]

Marvell, another considerable poet, also wrote a poem on the death of Oliver Cromwell. Marvell held office, during the Protectorate, as an assistant to John Milton and later became a member of parliament, in the reign of Charles II. The following is an extract, as the poem is a long one.

O Cromwell! Heaven's favourite, to none
Have such high honours from above been showne,
From whom the elements we mourners see,
And Heaven itself would the great herald be,
Which with more care set forth his obsequies
Than those of Moses, hid from humane eyes;
As jealous only here, lest all be lesse
Than we could to his memory expresse.
    Then let us too our course of mourning keep;
Where Heaven leads, 'tis piety to weep.
Stand back, ye seas, and shrunk beneath the vaile

[14] Andrew Marvell, "Poem upon the Death of O. C.," *The Poems and Letters of Andrew Marvell*, ed. H. M. Margoliouth (1962), I, 127–29.

Of your abysse, with cover'd head bewaile
Your monarch: we demand not your supplies
To compass-in our Isle,—our tears suffice,
Since him away the dismall tempest rent,
Who once more joyn'd us to the continent;
Who planted England on the Fland'rick shore,
And stretch'd our frontier to the Indian ore;
Whose greater truths obscure the fables old,
Whether of British saints or worthyes told;
And in a valour less'ning Arthur's deeds,
For holiness the Confessour exceeds.
    He first put arms into Religion's hand
And tim'rous conscience unto courage mann'd;
The soldier taught that inward mail to weare,
And fearing God, how they should nothing feare;
Those strokes, he said will pierce through all below,
Where those that strike from Heav'n fetch their blow.
Astonish'd armyes did their flight prepare,
And cityes strong were stormèd by his prayer;
Of that forever Preston's field shall tell
The story, and impregnable Clonmell.
And where the sandy mountain Fenwick scal'd,
The sea between, yet hence his pray'r prevail'd.
What man was ever so in Heav'n obeyed
Since the commanded sun o'er Gibeon stay'd?
In all his warrs needs must he triumph, when
He conquer'd God, still ere he fought with men:
Hence though in battle none so brave or fierce,
Yet him the adverse steel could never pierce;
Pity it seemed to hurt him more, that felt
Each wound himself which he to others delt,
Danger itself refusing to offend
So loose an enemy, so fast a friend.
Friendship, that sacred virtue, long does claime
The first foundation of his house and name:
But within one its narrow limits fall,
His tenderness extended unto all,
And that deep soule through every channell flows,
Where kindly Nature loves itself to lose.
More strong affections never reason serv'd,
Yet still affected most what best deserv'd.

If he Eliza lov'd to that degree,
(Though who more worthy to be lov'd than she?)
If so indulgent to his own, how deare
To him the children of the Highest were!
For her he once did Nature's tribute pay;
For these his life adventur'd every day;
And 'twould be found, could we his thoughts have cast,
Their griefs struck deepest, if Eliza's last.
What prudence more than human did he need
To keep so deare, so diff'ring minds agreed?
The worser sort, so conscious of their ill,
Lye weak and easy to the ruler's will;
But to the good (too many or too few)
All law is useless, all reward is due.
Oh! ill-advis'd, if not for love, for shame,
Spare yet your own, if you neglect his fame;
Lest others dare to think your zeal a maske,
And you to govern only Heaven's taske.
Valour, Religion, Friendship, Prudence dy'd
At once with him, and all that's good beside;
And we, Death's refuge, Nature's dregs, confin'd
To loathsome life, alas! are left behind.
Where we (so once we us'd) shall now no more,
To fetch day, presse about his chamber-door,
From which he issu'd with that awful state,
It seem'd Mars broke through Janus' double gate;
Yet always temper'd with an air so mild,
No April sunns, that e'er so gently smil'd;
No more shall heare that powerful language charm,
Whose force oft spar'd the labour of his arm;
No more shall follow where he spent the dayes
In warre, in counsell, or in pray'r and praise;
Whose meanest acts he would himself advance,
As ungirt David to the arke did dance.
All, all is gone of ours or his delight
In horses fierce, wild deer, or armour bright;
Francisca fair can nothing now but weep,
Nor with soft notes shall sing his cares asleep.

*Eliza was Elizabeth, reputedly Cromwell's favorite daughter,
who predeceased him. She died of cancer on August 6, 1658.*

LUCY HUTCHINSON: "WANTON WITH POWER" [15]

Lucy Hutchinson was the wife of a republican colonel who wrote, for the benefit of their children, memoirs of her husband's life and adventures. Hutchinson, who had been a member of Parliament, retired from public activities after Cromwell dismissed the Rump.

In the interim, Cromwell and his army grew wanton with their power, and invented a thousand tricks of government, which, when nobody opposed, they themselves fell to dislike and vary every day. First he calls a parliament out of his own pocket, himself naming a sort of godly men for every county, who meeting and not agreeing, a part of them, in the name of the people, gave up the sovereignty to him. Shortly after he makes up several sorts of mock parliaments, but not finding one of them absolutely for his turn, turned them off again. He soon quitted himself of his triumvirs, and first thrust out Harrison, then took away Lambert's commission, and would have been king but for fear of quitting his generalship. He weeded, in a few months' time, above a hundred and fifty godly officers out of the army, with whom many of the religious soldiers went off, and in their room abundance of the King's dissolute soldiers were entertained; and the army was almost changed from that godly religious army, whose valour God had crowned with triumph, into the dissolute army they had beaten, bearing yet a better name.

His wife and children were setting up for principality, which suited no better with any of them than scarlet upon the ape; only, to speak the truth of himself, he had much natural greatness, and well became the place he had usurped. His daughter Fleetwood was humbled, and not exalted with these things, but the rest were insolent fools. Claypole, who married his daughter, and his son Henry, were two debauched ungodly cavaliers. Richard was a peasant in his nature, yet gentle and virtuous, but became not greatness. His

[15] Lucy Hutchinson, *Memoirs of Colonel Hutchinson*, ed. C. H. Firth (1885), pp. 201–5.

court was full of sin and vanity, and the more abominable, because they had not yet quite cast away the name of God, but profaned it by taking it in vain upon them. True religion was now almost lost, even among the religious party, and hypocrisy became an epidemical disease, to the sad grief of Colonel Hutchinson, and all true-hearted Christians and Englishmen. Almost all the ministers everywhere fell in and worshipped this beast, and courted and made addresses to him. So did the city of London and many of the degenerate lords of the land, with the poor-spirited gentry. The Cavaliers, in policy, who saw that while Cromwell reduced all the exercise of tyrannical power under another name, there was a door opened for the restoring of their party, fell much in with Cromwell, and heightened all his disorders.

He at last exercised such an arbitrary power that the whole land grew weary of him, while he set up a company of silly, mean fellows, called major-generals, as governors in every county. These ruled according to their wills, by no law but what seemed good in their own eyes, imprisoning men, obstructing the course of justice between man and man, perverting right through partiality, acquitting some that were guilty, and punishing some that were innocent as guilty. Then he exercised another project to raise money, by decimation of the estates of all the king's party, of which action it is said Lambert was the instigator. At last he took upon himself to make lords and knights, and wanted not many fools, both of the army and gentry, to accept of and strut in his mock titles. Then the Earl of Warwick's grandchild and the Lord Falconbridge married his two daughters; such pitiful slaves were the nobles of those days. At last Lambert, perceiving himself to have been all this while deluded with hopes and promises of succession and seeing that Cromwell now intended to confirm the government in his own family, fell off from him; but behaved himself very pitifully and meanly, was turned out of all his places, and returned again to plot new vengeance at his house at Wimbledon, where he fell to dress his flowers in his garden, and work at the needle with his wife and his maids, while he was watching an opportunity to serve again his ambition, which had this difference from the Protector's: the one was gallant and great, the other had nothing but an unworthy pride, most isolent in prosperity and as abject and base in adversity.

The Cavaliers, seeing their victors thus beyond their hopes falling into their hands, had not the patience to stay till things ripened of themselves, but were every day forming designs and plotting for the murder of Cromwell, and other insurrections, which being contrived in drink and managed by false and cowardly fellows, were still revealed to Cromwell, who had most excellent intelligence of all things that passed, even in the King's closet; and by these unsuccessful plots they were only the obstructors of what they sought to advance, while, to speak the truth, Cromwell's personal courage and magnanimity upheld him against all enemies and malcontents. His own army disliked him, and once when sevenscore officers had combined to cross him in something he was pursuing, and engaged to one another, Lambert being the chief, with solemn promises and invocations to God, the Protector hearing of it, overawed them: "it was not they who upheld him, but he them," and rated them and made them understand what pitiful fellows they were: whereupon they all, like rated dogs, clapped their tails between their legs and begged his pardon, and left Lambert to fall alone, none daring to own him publicly, though many in their hearts wished him sovereignty.

GEORGE FOX: "HE THANKED ME AND BID ME GO TO HIS HOUSE" [16]

George Fox, the founder of the Society of Friends, met Cromwell on at least three occasions and recorded his experiences in his Journal. In 1654, he was arrested in Leicestershire and brought up to London by Captain Drury.

After Captain Drury lodged me at the Mermaid, he left me there, and went to give the Protector an account of me. When he came to see me again, he told me the Protector required that I should promise not to take up a carnal sword or weapon against

[16] George Fox, *Journal*, rev. by Norman Penney (1924), pp. 104–6, 173.

him or the government. And I should write it in what words I saw good, and set my hand to it. I said little in reply to Captain Drury. But next morning I was moved of the Lord to write a paper "To the Protector by the Name of Oliver Cromwell," wherein I did in the presence of the Lord God declare that I did deny the wearing or drawing of a carnal sword, or any other outward weapon, against all violence, and against the works of darkness; and to turn people from darkness to light; and to bring them from the occasion of war and fighting to the peaceable gospel, and from being evil-doers which the magistrates' swords should be a terror to. When I had written what the Lord had given me to write, I set my name to it, and gave it to Captain Drury to hand to Oliver Cromwell, which he did.

Then after some time Captain Drury brought me before the Protector himself at Whitehall. It was in a morning, before he was dressed, and one Harvey, who had come a little among the Friends, but was disobedient, waited upon him. When I came in, I was moved to say, "Peace be in this house"; and I bid him to keep in the fear of God, that he might receive wisdom from Him, that by it he might be directed, and order all things under his hand to God's glory. I spake much to him of Truth, and much discourse I had with him about religion; wherein he carried himself very moderately. But he said we quarrelled with priests, whom he called ministers. I told him I did not quarrel with them but they quarrelled with me and my friends. "But," said I, "if we own the prophets, Christ, and the apostles, we cannot hold up such teachers, prophets, and shepherds as the prophets, Christ and the apostles declared against; but we must declare against them by the same power and spirit." Then I shewed him that the prophets, Christ, and the apostles declared freely, and against them that did not declare freely, such as preached for filthy lucre, and divined for money, and preached for hire, and were covetous and greedy, like the dumb dogs that can never have enough; and that they that have the same spirit that Christ and the prophets and the apostles had, could not but declare against all such now, as they did then. As I spake, he several times said it was very good and it was truth. I told him that all Christendom (so called) possessed the Scriptures, but wanted the power and spirit that they had who gave forth the

Scriptures and that was the reason they were not in fellowship with the Son, or with the Father, or with the Scriptures, or with one another.

Many more words I had with him, but people coming in, I drew a little back; and as I was turning, he caught me by the hand, and, with tears in his eyes, said, "Come again to my house, for if thou and I were but an hour of a day together, we should be nearer one to the other"; adding that he wished me no more ill than he did his own soul. I told him if he did, he wronged his own soul; and I bid him hearken to God's voice, that he might stand in His counsel and obey it; and if he did so, that would keep him from hardness of heart; but if he did not hear God's voice, his heart would be hardened. He said it was true. . . .

During the time I was in London [in 1658] many services lay upon me; for it was a time of much suffering. I was moved to write to Oliver Cromwell, and lay before him the sufferings of Friends, both in this nation and in Ireland. There was also a talk about this time of making Cromwell king: whereupon I was moved to go to him. I met him in the Park and told him that they that would put him on a crown would take away his life. And he asked me what did I say. And I said again, they that sought to put him on a crown would take away his life; and I bid him mind the crown that was immortal. He thanked me, and bid me go to his house. Afterwards, I was moved to write to him more fully concerning that matter. . . .

[Later, in 1658] I went to Kingston, and thence to Hampton Court, to speak with the Protector about the sufferings of the Friends. I met him riding into Hampton Court Park, and before I came to him, as he rode at the head of his life-guard, I saw and felt a waft of death go forth against him; and when I came to him he looked like a dead man. After I had laid the sufferings of the Friends before him, and had warned him, according as I was moved to speak to him, he bid me come to his house. So I returned to Kingston, and next day went to Hampton Court, to speak further with him. But when I came he was very sick, and Harvey, who was the one that waited on him, told me the doctors were not willing I should speak with him. So I passed away, and never saw him more.

FRANCESCO GIAVARINA: CROMWELL'S LAST DAYS (1658) [17]

Francesco Giavarina was the Venetian Resident in England.

August 13: The Court is sad and sorrowful this week owing to the Protector's gout and to the death of his second daughter [Elizabeth] which occurred these last days [August 6] to the grief of her parents, relations, and the whole Court. The funeral took place the day before yesterday in the evening as the Protector did not wish there to be any pomp. . . .

August 20: The Protector is still a victim to the gout and this has recently been aggravated to the stone from which at times he suffers extremely. . . .

August 27: Whereas it seemed last week that the gout and stone from which the Protector was suffering was ceasing and the pain growing less, the Court has been grieved to see his illness change to tertian fever [malaria]. He is now suffering in mind and body, unable to attend to many affairs which require decision from his ripe and most acute intellect. Meanwhile his Highness returned on Tuesday to this city from Hampton Court. The palace of Whitehall is on the river and as it was feared that the air there generated by the water might be injurious to his health, they are preparing the house of St. James's some distance from the Thames, which in the time of kings was the residence of the Prince of Wales and since the change has been a barrack for soldiers. Cromwell proposed to reside there with his household to be farther away from what might harm him and prevent him from enjoying the health which is such a boon to all.

At the palace they speak of His Highness's illness as a light matter, but some outside, who profess to have authentic information and to know what is passing within, say that it is very dangerous, and some even assert that he has made his will and appointed his elder son Richard to be generalissimo of the land forces, High Ad-

---

[17] *Calendar of State Papers* (Venice), XXXI (1657–59), 236–42.

miral of the sea forces and Lord Warden of the Cinque ports, all supreme offices of the highest importance.

If the chief should die, and he is mortal like other men, disturbance and dissension will undoubtedly arise in this country. Neither of his sons is capable of taking the place that he has occupied, and if he nominates one of them before he passes away, as everyone expects, to be his successor, he being obliged to appoint one by act of parliament, there would not be the slightest difficulty in unseating him by others who aspire to this high dignity, especially as neither of the sons is popular with the troops or esteemed by them, while the soldiers retain their affection and respect for [General] Lambert. . . .

September 3: The illness of the Protector keeps the whole Court in anxiety. Accordingly nothing has happened of importance at the palace and nothing arrived this week from abroad. Letters from all parts are delayed as the wind these days has been very contrary and very high, so I have nothing of consequence to communicate. There is only the Protector's illness. On Saturday, Sunday, and Monday he was exceeding bad; and on Tuesday evening he was given up by the doctors. All of a sudden he became better, slept well that night, and the fever which should have recurred in the morning was very slight. He has remained in that state since, with little fever but extremely weak, but in spite of this it is hoped that he may soon recover. At the time when he seemed at his last gasp no one at Court showed himself and it was not possible to speak with anyone, but now, since he is better, everyone is visible, they all talk freely, rejoice, and look forward to his recovered health.

The improvement has certainly been sudden, unexpected, and extraordinary. Many think that it is not altogether a good sign, and recall that his daughter [Elizabeth] Claypole, at the height of her illness, had a similar respite, which did not prevent her succumbing to the violence of the paroxysms and paying the debt of nature. . . .

September 10: After sealing my last dispatch, I was informed His Highness had become so much worse about midday that three hours later he expired, after having governed this country about five years.

JOHN MAIDSTON: "A VAST TREASURY OF NATURAL PARTS" [18]

Maidston was Oliver Cromwell's cofferer, or steward.

His body was compact and strong, his stature under six foot (I believe about two inches), his head so shaped as you might see it a storehouse and shop both of a vast treasury of natural parts. His temper exceeding fiery, as I have known, but the flame of it kept down, for the most part, or soon allayed with those moral endowments he had. He was naturally compassionate to objects in distress, even to an effeminate measure; though God had given him a heart, wherein was left little room for any fear but what was due to Himself, of which there was a large proportion, yet did he exceed in tenderness towards sufferers. A larger soul, I think, hath seldom dwelt in a house of clay than his was.

I do believe, if his story were impartially transmitted, and the unprejudiced world well possessed with it, she would add him to her nine worthies and make up that number a *decemviri*. He lived and died in comfortable communion with God, as judicious persons near him well observed. He was that Mordecai that sought the welfare of his people and spake peace to his seed, yet were his temptations such, as it appeared frequently, that he that hath grace enough for many men, may have too little for himself; the treasure he had been but in an earthen vessel, and that equally defiled with original sin, as any other man's nature is.

SAMUEL CARRINGTON: "GENEROSITY, COURTESY, AFFABILITY" [19]

Samuel Carrington, who was Cromwell's earliest biographer, wrote about him immediately after he died. Possibly, however, his panegyric should be taken no more seriously than the ridiculous abuse and obvious embroideries of James Heath's Flagellum Or The Life, Birth and Burial of Oliver Cromwell

---

[18] *Thurloe State Papers*, I, 766.

[19] Samuel Carrington, *The History of the Life and Death of His most Serene Highness Oliver late Lord Protector* (1659), pp. 263–66.

The Late Usurper *(1663), which some writers on Cromwell have thought worth quoting extensively.*

To say any more of his generosity, this virtue he highly recommended above all others unto his Ministers of State and unto his ambassadors and unto his children; and whereof that noble Lady Claypole, his daughter of worthy memory, did give many evidences during his life and even at the article of her death, as that she thereby did beget tears in the most obstinate and hardiest enemies of this State [Heath said that "she threatened judgment like another mad Cassandra"]. A worthy daughter of so famous a father when Heaven too soon snatched away both from the virtuous and the miserable; and whose soul did admirably correspond with his fortune and the majesty of her comportment. How many of the royalist prisoners got she not freed? How many did she not save from death whom the laws condemned? How many persecuted Christians hath she not snatched out of the hands of the tormenters?—quite contrary unto that Herodias who could do anything with her father. She employed her prayers even with tears to spare such men whose ill fortune had designed them to suffer when as this grand hero being transported, as it were and even ravished to see his own image so lively described in those lovely and charming features of that winning sex, could refuse her nothing; insomuch that when his clemency and justice did balance the pardon of a poor criminal, this most charming advocate knew so skilfully to disarm him that, his sword falling out of his hands, his arms only served to lift her up from those knees on which she had cast herself, to wipe the tears and to embrace her. So likewise it is believed that this illustrious princess's precipitated death did not a little contribute to his late Highness's sickening . . . nor did he long outlive her.

Wherefore the generosity, courtesy and affability of his late Highness did so superabound as that no one person ever departed from his presence unsatisfied; for he received the petitions of all men, he heard their grievances and his charitable memory was so retentive as that he never forgot their requests, but made it his chief object to have them in mind and most tenderly provide for them.

He esteemed those he had overcome and took a delight to pardon them and to make them sharers of his fortune; provided that they would give over to make themselves unfortunate by their obstinacy. He was used to say that hearts were as well to be overcome as fortresses, and that the one were no more to be demolished than the other because they had belonged to other masters insomuch that he esteemed as a great conquest to have gained gallant men to his party.

THE EARL OF CLARENDON: "NOT A MAN OF BLOOD" [20]

As Sir Edward Hyde, the first Earl of Clarendon had been a fellow member of the House of Commons with Cromwell; and as a principal Minister of Charles II when he was in exile, Hyde was one of Cromwell's greatest enemies. In his famous book entitled the History of the Great Rebellion, *written after his ungrateful master had dismissed and exiled him, and not published until 1702, Clarendon has much to say about Cromwell.*

He was one of those men, whom not even his enemies can abuse without at the same time praising him; for he could never have done half that mischief without great parts of courage, industry and judgment. He must have had a wonderful understanding in the natures and humours of men, and as great a dexterity in applying them; who from a private and obscure birth (though of a good family) without interest of estate, alliance or friendship, could raise himself to such a height, and compound and knead such opposite and contradictory tempers, humours, and interests into a consistence that contributed to his designs and to their own destruction; whilst himself grew insensibly powerful enough to cut off those by whom he had climbed in the instant that they projected to demolish their own building. What Vellieus Paterculus said of Cinna may very justly be said of him: "he dared what no good man dared; he was able to achieve what had been achieved by no one

[20] G. D. Boyle, *Selections from Clarendon* (1889), pp. 277–78, 280, 283.

else except the bravest." Without doubt no man with more wickedness ever attempted anything or brought to pass what he desired more wickedly, more in the face and contempt of religion and moral honesty; yet wickedness as great as his could never have accomplished those trophies without the assistance of a great spirit, an admirable circumspection and sagacity and a most magnanimous resolution.

When he appeared first in the parliament, he seemed to have a person in no degree gracious, no ornament of discourse, none of those talents which use to reconcile the affections of the stander-by: yet as he grew into place and authority, his parts seemed to be raised, as if he had had concealed faculties, till he had occasion to use them; and when he was to act the part of a great man, he did it without any independence, notwithstanding the want of custom.

After he was confirmed and invested Protector by the Humble Petition and Advice, he consulted with very few upon any action of importance nor communicated any enterprise he resolved upon with more than those who were to have principal parts in the execution of it; nor with them sooner than was absolutely necessary. When he once resolved, in which he was not rash, he would not be dissuaded from nor endure any contradiction of his power and authority; but extorted obedience from them who were not willing to yield it. . . .

To reduce three nations, which perfectly hated him, to an entire obedience to all his dictates; to awe and govern those nations by an army that was undevoted to him and wished his ruin, was an instance of his prodigious address. But his greatness at home was but a shadow of the glory he had abroad. It was hard to discover which feared him most, France, Spain or the Low Countries, where his friendship was current at the value he put upon it. As they did all sacrifice their honour and interest to his pleasure, so there is nothing he could have demanded that either of them would have denied him. . . .

He was not a man of blood and totally declined Machiavel's method, which prescribes, upon any alteration of government, as a thing absolutely necessary to cut off all the heads of those, and extirpate their families, who are friends to the old one. It was confidently reported that in the council of officers it was more than once proposed "that there might be a general massacre of all the royal party as the only expedient to secure the government," but that Cromwell would never consent to it; it may be, out of too much contempt of his enemies. In a word, as he had all the wickedness against which damnation is denounced and for which hell-fire is prepared, so he had some virtues which have caused the memory of some men in all ages to be celebrated; and he will be looked upon by posterity as a brave bad man.

PART THREE

CROMWELL IN HISTORY

In his essay "The Fame of Cromwell" and in his bibliography of writings about Cromwell, the late Wilbur Cortez Abbott indicated the vast range of comments from innumerable pens, some steeped in acid, and some filled with as much ignorance as imagination. Thomas Carlyle, describing, in the middle of the nineteenth century what had appeared during the two hundred years or so that followed Cromwell's death, referred to the material as "bewildered, interminable rubbish heaps . . . the dreariest perhaps that anywhere exist still visited by human curiosity." Nevertheless, it is considerably interesting and indeed amusing (especially for those who do not believe that history is an exact science) to observe how opinions about Cromwell have varied and oscillated, even after Carlyle's rescuing the memory of this Christian statesman from the depths of prejudice. In Abbott's essay and in the first chapter of my own book, The Greatness of Oliver Cromwell, *the historiography of the subject is summarized and analyzed. In the following pages I quote a selection of views, ranging from the confident assertions of the so-called historians of the Age of Enlightenment to the scientific analysts of the twentieth-century universities.*

DAVID HUME: "EVEN A SUPERIOR GENIUS" (1754) [1]

David Hume was a distinguished Scottish philosopher, whose History of England *was a money-maker.*

It seems to me, that the circumstances of Cromwell's life, in which his abilities are principally discovered, is his rising from a private station, in opposition to so many rivals, so much advanced

---

[1] David Hume, *History of England* (ed. 1841), V, 409–11.

before him, to a high command and authority in the army. His great courage and address were all requisite for this important acquisition. Yet will not this promotion appear the effect of supernatural abilities, when we consider that Fairfax himself, a private gentleman, who had not the advantage of a seat in parliament, had, through the same steps, attained even superior rank, and, if endued with common capacity and penetration, had been able to retain it. To incite such an army to rebellion against the parliament, required no uncommon art or industry: to have kept them in obedience had been the more difficult enterprise.

When the breach was once formed between the military and civil powers, a supreme and absolute authority, from that moment is devolved on the general; and if he be afterwards pleased to employ artifice or policy, it may be regarded, on most occasions, as great condescension, if not as superfluous caution. That Cromwell was ever able really to blind or over-reach either the king or the republicans, does not appear: As they possessed no means of resisting the force under his command, they were glad to temporize with him, and, by seeming to be deceived, wait for opportunities of freeing themselves from his dominion. If he deluded the military fanatics, it is to be considered, that their interests and his evidently concurred, that their ignorance and low education exposed them to the grossest imposition, and that he himself was at bottom as frantic an enthusiast as the worst of them, and, in order to obtain their confidence, needed but to display those vulgar and ridiculous habits, which he had early acquired, and on which he set so high a value. An army is so forcible, and at the same time so coarse a weapon, that any hand which wields it, may, without much dexterity, perform any operation, and attain any ascendant in human society.

The domestic administration of Cromwell, though it discovers great abilities, was conducted without any plan either of liberty or arbitrary power: Perhaps, his difficult situation admitted of neither. His foreign enterprises, though full of intrepidity were pernicious to the national interest, and seem more the result of impetuous fury or narrow prejudices, than of cool foresight and deliberation. An eminent personage, however, he was in many respects, and even a superior genius; but unequal and irregular in his operations. And though not defective in any talent, except that of elocution, the abilities, which in him were most admirable, and which contributed to his marvellous success, were the magnanimous resolution of his enterprises, and practising on the weaknesses of mankind.

If we survey the moral character of Cromwell with that indulgence which is due to the blindness and infirmities of the human species, we shall not be inclined to load his memory with such violent reproaches as those which his enemies usually throw upon it. Amidst the passions and prejudices of that period, that he should prefer the parliamentary to the royal cause, will not appear extraordinary; since, even at present some men of sense and knowledge are disposed to think that the question, with regard to the justice of the quarrel, may be regarded as doubtful and uncertain. The murder of the king, the most atrocious of all his actions, was to him covered under a mighty cloud of republican and fanatical illusions; and it is not impossible, but that he might believe it, as many others did, the most meritorious action he could perform.

His subsequent usurpation was the effect of necessity, as well as of ambition; nor is it easy to see how the various factions could at that time have been restrained, without a mixture of military and arbitrary authority. The private deportment of Cromwell as a son, a husband, a father, a friend, is exposed to no considerable censure, if it does not rather merit praise. And, upon the whole, his character does not appear more extraordinary and unusual by the mixture of so much absurdity with so much penetration, than by his tempering such violent ambition and such enraged fanaticism with so much regard to justice and humanity.

TOBIAS SMOLLETT: "ENTHUSIASM, HYPOCRISY, AMBITION" (1758) [2]

Smollett was the famous novelist whose History of England *was written in rivalry to Hume's.*

Oliver was of a robust make and constitution, and his aspect was manly though clownish. His education extended no farther

[2] Tobias Smollett, *History of England* (ed. 1759), VII, 446–48.

than a superficial knowledge of the Latin tongue; but he inherited great talents from nature; though they were such as he could not have exerted to advantage at any other juncture than that of a civil war inflamed by religious contests. His character was formed from an amazing conjunction of enthusiasm, hypocrisy, and ambition. He was possessed of courage and resolution that overlooked all danger and saw no difficulty. He dived into the characters of mankind with a wonderful sagacity; while he concealed his own purposes under the impenetrable shield of dissimulation. He reconciled the most atrocious crimes to the most rigid notions of religious obligation. From the severest exercise of devotion he relaxed into the most ludicrous and idle buffoonery. He preserved the dignity and distance of his character in the midst of the coarsest familiarity. He was cruel and tyrannical from policy; just and temperate from inclination: perplexed and despicable in his discourse; clear and consummate in his designs: ridiculous in his reveries; respectable in his conduct: in a word, the strangest compound of villainy and virtue, baseness and magnanimity, absurdity and good sense, that we find upon record in the annals of mankind.

THOMAS CARLYLE: "A MAN OF TRUTHS" (1845) [3]

It was Carlyle, whose edition of The Letters and Speeches *of Oliver Cromwell was first published in October, 1845, and proved a great success, who helped to get rid of the notion, so popular in the eighteenth century, that Cromwell was a villain and a hypocrite.*

These authentic utterances of the man Oliver himself—I have gathered them from far and near; fished them up from the foul Lethean quagmires where they lay buried; I have washed, or endeavoured to wash them clean from foreign stupidities (such a job

---

[3] S. C. Lomas, ed., *The Letters and Speeches of Oliver Cromwell with Elucidations by Thomas Carlyle* (1904), I, 10–11.

of buckwashing as I do not long to repeat); and the world shall now see them in their own shape. Working for long years in those unspeakable Historic Provinces, of which the reader has already had account, it became more and more apparent to one that this man Oliver Cromwell was, as the popular fancy represents him, the soul of the Puritan Revolt, without whom it had never been a revolt transcendantly memorable, and an Epoch in the World's History; that in fact he, more than is common in such cases, does deserve to give his name to the Period in question, and have the Puritan Revolt considered as a Cromwelliad, which issue is already very visible for it. And then, farther, altogether contrary to the popular fancy, it becomes apparent that this Oliver was not a man of falsehoods, but a man of truths; whose words do carry a meaning with them, and above all others of that time are worth considering. His words,—and still more his *silences,* and unconscious instincts, when you have spelt and lovingly deciphered these also out of his words,—will in several ways reward the study of an earnest man. An earnest man, I apprehend, may gather from these words of Oliver's, were there even no other evidence, that of the character of Oliver, and of the affairs he worked in, is much of the reverse of that mad jumble of "hypocrisies," & c. & c., which at present passes current as such.

But certainly, on any hypothesis as to that, such a set of Documents may hope to be elucidative in various respects. Oliver's Character, and that of Oliver's Performance in this world: here best of all may we expect to read it, whatsoever it was. Even if false, these words, authentically spoken and written by the chief actor in the business, must be of prime moment for understanding of it. These are the words this man found suitablest to represent the Things themselves, around him, and in him, of which we seek a History. The newborn Things and Events, as they bodied themselves forth to Oliver Cromwell from the Whirlwind of passing Time,—this is the name and definition he saw good to give of them. To get at these direct utterances of his, is to get at the very heart of the business; were there once light for us in these, the business had begun again at the heart of it to be luminous!

FRANÇOIS PIERRE GUILLAUME GUIZOT: "HIS REAL OBJECT UNATTAINED" (1854) [4]

Three practicing statesmen wrote books about Oliver Cromwell: Guizot, who was Prime Minister of France, Theodore Roosevelt, who was President of the United States of America, and Lord Morley, who was a member of the British Cabinet until 1914. There are also some observations by Winston Churchill, who thought that Cromwell was a "cloudy soul" and disliked him as a Puritan and a dictator. The following is Guizot's view; those of Roosevelt and Morley appear on later pages.

Cromwell died in the plenitude of his power and greatness. He had succeeded beyond all expectation, far more than any other of those men has succeeded, who, by their genius, have raised themselves, as he had done, to supreme authority; for he had attempted and accomplished, with equal success, the most opposite designs. During eighteen years he had been an ever-victorious actor on the world's stage, he had alternately sown disorder and established order, effected and punished revolution, overthrown and restored government, in his country. At every moment, under all circumstances, he had distinguished with admirable sagacity the dominant interests and passions of the time, so as to make them the instruments of his own rule,—careless whether he belied his antecedent conduct, so long as he triumphed in concert with the popular instinct, and explaining the inconsistencies of his conduct by the ascendant unity of his power. He is, perhaps, the only example which history affords of one man having governed the most opposite events, and proved sufficient for the most varied destinies. And in the course of his violent and changeful career, incessantly exposed to all kinds of enemies and conspiracies, Cromwell experienced this crowning favour of fortune, that his life was never actually attacked; the sovereign against whom Killing had been declared to be No Murder, never found himself face to face with an

---

[4] F. P. G. Guizot, *Cromwell and the English Commonwealth*, trans. Andrew R. Scoble (1854), II, 406–8.

assassin. The world has never known another example of success at once so constant and so various, or of fortune so invariably favourable, in the midst of such manifold conflicts and perils.

Yet Cromwell's death-bed was clouded with gloom. He was unwilling not only to die, but also, and most of all, to die without having attained his real and final object. However great his egotism may have been, his soul was too great to rest satisfied with the highest fortune, if it were merely personal, and, like himself, of ephemeral earthly duration. Weary of the ruin he had caused, it was his cherished wish to restore to his country a regular and stable government—the only government which was suited to its wants, a monarchy under the control of parliament. And at the same time, with an ambition which extended beyond the grave, under the influence of that thirst for permanence which is the stamp of true greatness, he aspired to leave his name and race in possession of the throne. He failed in both designs: his crimes had raised up obstacles against him, which neither his prudent genius nor his persevering will could surmount; and though covered, as far as he himself was concerned with power and glory, he died with his dearest hopes frustrated, and leaving behind him, as his successors, the two enemies whom he had so ardently combatted—anarchy and the Stuarts.

God does not grant to those great men, who have laid the foundations of their greatness amidst disorder and revolution, the power of regulating, at their pleasure, and for succeeding ages, the government of nations.

LEOPOLD VON RANKE: THREE GREAT ACHIEVEMENTS (1875) [5]

Von Ranke was the father of "scientific history" who devoted much of his life to the study of European history in the seventeenth century.

It was among a lower class, among the freeholders in the various counties, the descendants of the Danes and Saxons, who formed

[5] Leopold Von Ranke, *A History of England principally in the Seventeenth Century* (Oxford: The Clarendon Press, 1875), IV, 106–11.

a counterpoise to the influence of the gentry, that he [Cromwell] sought his allies. It was on the interest of this class especially that the association was based which rendered the eastern counties the most powerful bulwark of the parliamentary party.

From the same class it was that Cromwell when the war broke out, in virtue of a commission granted him by Lord Essex, levied the body of cavalry to which he owed his great successes. They were men of sufficient means to be independent of pay, and whose bodily powers had been tried and developed by agricultural labour. But it was necessary that they should also be men of personal courage. Cromwell tested the squadron while yet in the course of formation by a sudden surprise, and dismissed those who then showed cowardice. They had to perform the meanest services, to sleep in the straw by their horses, and to groom them carefully: for all depended upon the good condition of their horses and the brightness and sharpness of their arms. Above all things they were bound by the strictest discipline. To the cavalry that Prince Rupert had organized among the Cavaliers, which won fame in the several battles and filled the land with the terror of their name, Cromwell desired to oppose a troop as brave, as serviceable, and as eager for victory. He saw that the strength of his enemies lay chiefly in the principle of honour; a principle which, according to medieval notions, is bound up with dutiful service and personal allegiance. This it was essential to confront by another, which should be equally powerful. His followers were all united by the same religious tendencies which harmonized with his own; they were as zealous separatists as their leader himself. They fought not so much for the rights of parliament, which still left room for doubting whether a man could bear arms against his hereditary sovereign, as for complete religious freedom and social equality. It was a confederation of men inspired by a fanaticism at once religious and political, but yet whose minds were schooled by discussion of the great controversies which had engrossed attention in the last few years, respecting the relations between prince and people, between the Episcopal Church and the sects, and who were now consolidated by a strict discipline into a military force. Shouting a psalm they threw themselves upon the enemy in the name of the Almighty; they granted no quarter; at times they were seen to retreat, but it was only to return to the attack with the greater vehemence: none of them would ever have taken refuge in flight: in most cases they remained masters of the field. In a short time Cromwell's Ironsides were reckoned a force of irresistible valour. The fame of their achievements roused those throughout the country who were like-minded to join their ranks, and to make their own the cause which they fondly believed was the cause of God.

Now that the great religious and political struggle was to be decided by the issues of war, it is clear what a position a member of parliament enjoyed who was at the same time the leader of so powerful and active a force.

Are we then to say that from the first it was Cromwell's design to secure for himself the supreme power?—a question which can scarcely be asked, and which certainly cannot be answered hastily. The consciousness of a high mission which animated him may have been strengthened and elevated by subsequent events; but to trace all his actions in detail to a settled plan is to be guilty of a false pragmatism which only obscures the motives which were really most powerful. He himself said on one occasion, "He goes furthest who knows not whither he is going." The directing impulse to all that he did or left undone was supplied in most cases by the necessities of the moment. His intention always was to break through the hostile forces which opposed him, and to overcome them by stratagem as much as by open war. To award him the merit of perfect sincerity, a praise which perhaps no single statesman of his day can rightfully claim, would be to over-estimate the value of the grandiloquent expressions in which he delighted. At times the real nature of his opinions is lost in a crowd of antitheses, at others he changes his tactics. The party which gathered round him and gave him importance in its turn imposed duties upon him, yet not always without reserve did he share their views.

Speaking strictly, there are three great achievements which established his personal influence. They all bear the stamp of self-defence necessitated by circumstances, of prompt resolution and a preparedness which was always ready for any reverse.

The first is the reorganization of the army in the years 1644–45. It was the moment at which Cromwell, in spite of, or rather in consequence of, his services at Marston Moor, since these procured him so large a following, was in danger of being ruined by the Scottish Presbyterian league, to which belonged the foremost men of the state and army. To meet this danger he carried the Self-Denying ordinance. In this was found the most effective means of removing the Grandees from the army, and depriving them as well as others of his opponents of their chief source of influence. We are surprised and shocked to find that it was necessary to employ a religious pretext to recommend and carry through a party measure. Still more startling is the fact that one man only was excepted from its application, and that man the one who had been its author. Whether or not such was his conscious intention from the first who can decide? There is a foresight of consequence which is more properly a presentiment than a deliberate intention.

The great exceptional stations in the world are not usually won by slow degrees. Ambition fixes its hopes upon them more from a half-instinctive feeling than with any settled design. At the decisive moment they suddenly offer themselves and are at once grasped. By the victory of Naseby Cromwell became master of England. Who would have ventured to accuse him of a breach of law while he advanced from victory to victory and decided a great struggle in which the nation had been engaged with all its might and soul? He was not the commander-in-chief of the army, and in parliament was nothing more than a simple member; but he ruled the former through the credit he had gained with it and his personal reputation, and through it he exercised a directing influence over the latter. Thanks to the double foundation on which it rested, his position was one of unrivalled strength. At one blow he had become the most powerful man in England.

Such an authority as this inevitably struggles to gain for itself a full and free development, which the forces kept in subjection by it, but not as yet entirely crushed, necessarily oppose. The Presbyterians and the King endeavoured to combine against him. The second great epoch in Cromwell's career is marked by his dissolution of the alliance and his final defeat of both parties. With the zealous Presbyterians, who regarded him as their sworn foe, he could never have come to an understanding: such an understanding seemed more feasible with the King, whose views on religious tolerance met his own demands. Cromwell showed sympathy for him, made him promises, inspired him with confidence, engaged in serious negotiations with him. But two conditions were required to bring the matter to a conclusion. In the first place it was essential that the army should agree to the advances, and next it was necessary that the King should not only promise them security against any reaction, but also the continuance of their privileged position in the country. But . . . the General himself by his negotiations fell under the suspicions of the army, which was deeply penetrated with democratic ideas; he was thought to be seeking some sort of agreement to provide for his own greatness and the future of his family. So far as the King was concerned it was no longer possible to obtain for him a recognition of an independent establishment for the army. Whatever promises Cromwell may have made, he gradually turned from him in open enmity. Cromwell was not without appreciation of the principles of monarchy, but he was entirely destitute of sympathy with what is called loyalty. He has told us that he would as readily fire his pistol in battle at the King as at any other foe. He did not hate Charles I, but he felt no scruple in destroying him when circumstances made it necessary. In his eyes it was allowable in urgent cases to overthrow the ruling powers. The ordinance of God he regarded only as the source of all authority; what form and fashion it might take was, he considered, left to human judgment. Cromwell did not start, like the Agitators, from the idea of the sovereignty of the people, but from the requirements of the common good. As to what was profitable or hurtful to the state, on that point each might judge for himself. The interest of good people was the common interest of all; to secure it, it was lawful to overthrow an established government; those whose intentions were perverse could be met by stratagem. These were the principles which may serve to justify all rebellion and violence: they are well suited to the position of a powerful ruler just rising into authority and casting all scruples behind him.

If Cromwell however entertained the design of overthrowing the monarchy, it was necessary that those Parliamentarians should also fall who had attempted to enter into an agreement with it, had they been formerly friends of his own or not. He declared it to be a religious duty—for solely to their daily increasing fury against the elect of God did he attribute their conduct—to purify the

Parliament from them. The Upper House was abolished; the King beheaded; in the Lower House, which now assumed the title of Parliament, those only were to be tolerated who were like-minded and as devoid of loyalty, and who followed his bidding. But that they should be tolerated for long was not to be expected. Far from obeying his lead, they claimed to be the supreme authority, to which the army ought rather to submit. Thus when Cromwell returned from the campaigns which had everywhere crushed all resistance to the Commonwealth and secured the recognition of its authority, how was he to allow the possession of the power he had himself founded to remain in the hands of men who sought to prescribe laws for him, and to place restrictions upon his authority? Cromwell openly uttered reproaches which personally affected the members, and would have cost them their popularity. But that was not his ultimate reason. There is some truth in the royalist charge that he had got rid of them in order not himself to be overthrown by them: and how, under any conditions, could a military and civil authority, with equal claims, have continued to rule side by side with each other? It was inevitable that they should quarrel; and in the quarrel the General necessarily gained the advantage, not only because he was the stronger of the two, but also because he had contributed the most to the establishment of the whole existing arrangements.

Here as ever the contradiction manifested itself between the intention as at first avowed and its subsequent results.

SAMUEL RAWSON GARDINER: "THE MAN GREATER THAN HIS WORK" (1899) [6]

Gardiner, who devoted most of his life to pioneering research into seventeenth-century British history, is said to have been an indirect descendant of Cromwell. He once said of Cromwell: "He stands forth as the typical Englishman of the modern world. . . . It is time for us to regard him as he really was, with all his physical and moral audacity, with all

⁶ Samuel Rawson Gardiner, *Oliver Cromwell* (New York: Collier Books, 1962), pp. 217–20.

his tenderness and spiritual yearnings, in the world of action what Shakespeare was in the world of thought, the greatest because the most typical Englishman of all time." One doubts if this sentence could be written in the second half of the twentieth century.

The man—it is ever so with the noblest—was greater than his work. In his own heart lay the resolution to subordinate self to public ends, and to subordinate material to moral and spiritual objects of desire. His work was accomplished under the conditions to which all human effort is subject. He was limited by the defects which make imperfect the character and intellect even of the noblest and wisest of mankind. He was limited still more by the unwillingness of his contemporaries to mould themselves after his ideas. The blows that he had struck against the older system had their enduring effects. Few wished for the revival of the absolute kingship, of the absolute authority of a single House of Parliament, or of the Laudian system of governing the Church.

In the early part of his career Oliver was able to say with truth of his own position: "No one rises so high as he who knows not whither he is going." The living forces of England—forces making for the destruction of those barriers which he himself was breaking through, buoyed him up—as a strong and self-confident swimmer, he was carried forward on the flowing tide. In the latter portion of the Protector's career it was far otherwise. His failure to establish a permanent government was due not merely to his deficiency in constructive imagination. It was due rather to two causes: the umbrage taken at his position as head of an army whose interference in political affairs gave even more offence than the financial burdens it imposed on a people unaccustomed to regular taxation; and the reaction which set in against the spiritual claims of that Puritanism of which he had become the mouthpiece. The first cause of offence needs no further comment. As for the second, it is necessary to lay aside all sectarian preoccupations, if ever a true historic judgment is to be formed. It was no reaction against the religious doctrine or ecclesiastical institutions upheld by the Protector that brought about the destruction of his system of government. It is in the highest degree unlikely that a revolution would ever have taken place merely to restore episcopacy or the Book of Common Prayer. So far as the reaction was not directed against militarism, it was directed against the introduction into the political world of what appeared to be too high a standard of morality, a reaction which struck specially upon Puritanism, but which would have struck with as much force upon any other form of religion which, like that upheld by Laud, called in the power of the State to enforce its claims.

Nor is this all that can be said. Even though Oliver was in his own person no sour fanatic, as royalist pamphleteers after the Restoration falsely asserted; it is impossible to deny that he strove by acts of government to lead men into the paths of morality and religion beyond the limit which average human nature had fixed for itself. In dealing with foreign nations his mistake on this head was more conspicuous, because he had far less knowledge of the conditions of efficient action abroad than he had at home. It may fairly be said that he knew less of Scotland than of England, less of Ireland than of Great Britain, and less of the Continent than any one of the three nations over which he ruled. It has sometimes been said that Oliver made England respected in Europe. It would be more in accordance with truth to say that he made her feared . . .

Oliver's claim to greatness can be tested by the undoubted fact that his character receives higher and wider appreciation as the centuries pass by. The limitations on his nature—the one-sidedness of his religious zeal, the mistakes of his policy—are thrust out of sight, the nobility of his motives, the strength of his character, and the breadth of his intellect, force themselves on the minds of generations for which the objects for which he strove have been for the most part attained, though often in a different fashion from that which he placed before himself. Even those who refuse to waste a thought on his spiritual aims remember with gratitude his constancy of effort to make England great by land and sea; and it would be well for them also to be reminded of his no less constant efforts to make England worthy of greatness.

JOHN MORLEY: "HIS IDEALS WERE HIGH . . . HIS AMBITION PURE" (1900) [7]

Even more than Carlyle's or Gardiner's, Morley's view of Cromwell is consonant with what we think of as the outlook of "the great Victorians," men of upright character and stern morals who coupled Cromwell with Gladstone in their pantheon of statesmen-heroes. Morley's biography of Cromwell, like Gardiner's, was written to commemorate the three hundredth anniversary of the Puritan statesman's birth, in 1599.

It is hard to resist the view that Cromwell's revolution was the end of the medieval rather than the beginning of the modern era. He certainly had little of the faith in Progress that became the inspiration of a later age. His respect for Public Opinion, supposed to be the driving force of modern government, was a strictly limited regard. In one sense he was no democrat, for he declared, as we have seen, that the question is not what pleases the people, but what is for their good. This came rather near to Charles's words as he stood upon the scaffold, that the people's liberty lay in the laws, "not their having a share in government; that is nothing pertaining to them." But then, on the other hand, Cromwell was equally strong that things obtained by force, though never so good in themselves, are both less to the ruler's honour and less likely to last. "What we gain in a free way, it is better than twice as much in a forced, and will be more truly ours and our posterity's"; and the safest test of any constitution is its acceptance by the people. And again, "It will be found an unjust and unwise jealousy to deprive a man of his natural liberty upon a supposition that he may abuse it." The root of all external freedom is here.

In saying that Cromwell had the spirit, insight, and grasp that fit a man to wield power in the greatest affairs, we only repeat that he had the instinct of government, and this is a very different thing from either a taste for abstract ideas of politics, or the passion

[7] John Morley, *Oliver Cromwell* (London: Macmillan & Co., Ltd., 1900), pp. 492–96.

for liberty. The instinct of order has been as often the gift of a
tyrant as of a hero, as common to some of the worst hearts in
human history as to some of the best. Cromwell was no Frederick
the Great, who spoke of mankind as *diese verdammte Race,* that
accursed tribe. He belonged to the rarer and nobler type of governing men, who see the golden side, who count faith, pity, hope,
among the counsels of practical wisdom, and who for political
power must ever seek a moral base. This is a key to men's admiration for him. His ideals were high, his fidelity to them though
sometimes clouded was still abiding, his ambition was pure. Yet it
can hardly be an accident that has turned him into one of the
idols of the school who hold shyly as yet in England but nakedly
in Germany, that might is a token of right, and that the strength
and power of the State is an end that tests and justifies all means.

When it is claimed that no English ruler did more than Cromwell
to shape the future of the land he governed, we run some risk of
straining history only to procure incense for retrograde ideals. Many
would contend that Thomas Cromwell in deciding the future of
one of the most powerful standing institutions of the country,
exercised a profounder influence than Oliver. Then if Cromwell
did little to shape the future of the church of England, neither did
he shape the future of the parliament of England. On the side of
constitutional construction, unwelcome as it may sound, a more
important place belongs to the sage and steadfast, though rather
unheroic Walpole. The development of the English constitution
has in truth proceeded on lines that Cromwell profoundly disliked.
The idea of a parliament always sitting and actively reviewing the
details of administration, was in his sight an intolerable mischief.
It was almost the only system against which his supple mind, so
indifferent as it was to all constitutional forms, stood inflexible.
Yet this for good or ill is our system today, and the system of the
wide host of political communities that have followed our parliamentary model. When it is said again that it was owing to Cromwell that Nonconformity had time to take such a deep root as to
defy the storm of the Restoration, do we not overlook the original
strength of all those giant puritan fibres from which both the
Rebellion and Cromwell himself had sprung? It was not a man,

not even such a man as Oliver, it was the same underlying spiritual forces which made the Rebellion, that also held fast against the Restoration. It would hardly be more forced to say that Cromwell was the founder of Nonconformity.

It has been called a common error of our day to ascribe far too much to the designs and the influence of eminent men, of rulers, and of government. The reproach is just and should impress us. The momentum of past events, the spontaneous impulses of the mass of a nation or a race, the pressure of general hopes and fears, the new things learned in the onward and diversified motions of "the great spirit of human knowledge," all have more to do with the progress of the world's affairs, than the deliberate views of even the most determined and far-sighted of its individual leaders. Thirty years after the death of the Protector a more successful revolution came about. The law was made more just, the tribunals were purified, the rights of conscience received at least a partial recognition, the press began to enjoy a freedom for which Milton had made a glorious appeal but which Cromwell never dared concede. Yet the Declaration of Right and the Toleration Act issued from a stream of ideas and maxims, aims and methods, that were not puritan. New tributaries had already swollen the volume and changed the currents of that broad confluence of manners, morals, government, belief, on whose breast Time guides the voyages of mankind. The age of Rationalism with its bright lights and sobering shadows had begun. Some ninety years after 1688 another revolution followed in the England across the Atlantic, and the gulf between Cromwell and Jefferson is measure of the vast distance that the minds of men had travelled. With the death of Cromwell, though the free churches remained as nurseries of stronghearted civil feeling, the brief life of puritan theocracy in England expired. It was a phase of a movement that left an inheritance of many noble thoughts, the memory of a brave struggle for human freedom, and a procession of strenuous master-spirits with Milton and Cromwell at their head. Political ends miscarry, and the revolutionary leader treads a path of fire. It is our true wisdom to learn how to combine sane and equitable historic verdicts on the event, with a just value in our study of the actor for those eternal qualities of high endeavour, on which amid limitless change in fashion, formula, direction, standard, and ideal, in all times and places the world's best hopes depend.

THEODORE ROOSEVELT: NEITHER A WASHINGTON NOR A NAPOLEON (1900) [8]

Roosevelt was forty-two and Governor of New York when his biography of Cromwell was published.

If Cromwell had been a Washington, the Puritan Revolution might have been permanent. His early acts, after the dissolution of the Long Parliament, showed a sincere desire on his part, and on the part of those whose leader he was, to provide some form of government which should secure justice and order, without leaving everything to the will of one man. His first effort was to summon an assembly of Puritan notables. In the interim he appointed a new Council of State with himself as Captain-General at its head. The fleet, the army, and the Independents generally, all hastened to pledge him their support, and England undoubtedly acquiesced in his action, being chiefly anxious to see whether or not the new Assembly could formulate a permanent scheme of government. If the Assembly and Cromwell together could have done this—that is, could have done work like that of the great Convention of the United States—all would have gone well.

In criticizing Cromwell, however, we must remember that generally in such cases an even greater share of blame must attach to the nation than to the man. Free government is only for nations that deserve it; and they lose all right to it by licentiousness, no less than by servility. If a nation cannot govern itself, it makes comparatively little difference whether its inability springs from slavish and craven distrust of its own powers, or from sheer incapacity on the part of its citizens to exercise self-control and to act together. Self-governing freemen must have the power to accept compromises, to make necessary concessions, each sacrificing somewhat of prejudice, or even of principle, and every group must show

[8] Theodore Roosevelt, *Oliver Cromwell* (1900), pp. 188–91, 219–25.

the necessary subordination of its particular interests to the interests of the community as a whole. When the people will not or cannot work together; when they permit groups of extremists to decline to accept anything that does not coincide with their own extreme views; or when they let power slip from their hands through sheer supine indifference; then they have themselves chiefly to blame if the power is grasped by stronger hands.

Yet, while keeping all this in mind, it must not be forgotten that a great and patriotic leader may, if the people have any capacity for self-government whatever, help them upwards along their hard path by his wise leadership, his wise yielding to even what he does not like, and his wise refusal to consider his own selfish interests. A people thoroughly unfit for self-government, as were the French at the end of the eighteenth century, are the natural prey of a conscienceless tyrant like Napoleon. A people like the Americans of the same generation can be led along the path of liberty and order by a Washington. The English people, in the middle of the seventeenth century, might have been helped to entire self-government by Cromwell, but were not sufficiently advanced politically to keep him from making himself their absolute master if he proved morally unequal to rising to the Washington level; though doubtless they would not have tolerated a man of the Napoleonic type. . . .

[On toleration] he was far in advance of his fellow Englishmen. He described their attitude perfectly, and indeed the attitude of all Europe, when he remarked: "Every sect saith, Oh, give me liberty! but given it and to spare, he will not yield it to any one else. Liberty of conscience is a natural right, and he that would have it ought to give it. . . . I have desired it from my heart; I have prayed for it; I have watched for the day to see union and right understanding between the godly people—Scots, English, Jews, Gentiles, Presbyterians, Independents, Anabaptists, and all."

The whole principle of religious toleration is summed up in these brief sentences. In his higher and better moments, and far more than most men of his generation, Cromwell tried to live up to them. When Mazarin, the great French cardinal, in responding to Cromwell's call for the toleration of the Vaudois, asked toleration for English Catholics, Cromwell answered truly, that he had done all he could in face of the hostile spirit of the people, and more

than had before been done in England. Of course the position of
the English Catholics was beyond all comparison better than that
of the Vaudois; but in such a controversy the ugly fact was that
neither side would grant to others what it demanded for itself.
To the most persecuted of all peoples Cromwell did render a
signal service. He connived at the settlement of Jews in London,
after having in vain sought to bring about their open toleration.

In Scotland, the rule of the Protector wrought unmixed good.
There was no persecution in so far as restraint of persecution and
intolerance could itself be called such. . . . In Ireland the case was
different . . . the great central fact remains that his Irish policy
was one of bitter oppression and that the abhorrence with which
the Irish, to this day, speak of "the curse of Crummle," is his-
torically justifiable.

It is a relief to turn from the Cromwellian policy in Ireland to
the Cromwellian policy in foreign affairs. England never stood
higher in her relations with the outside world than she stood under
Cromwell.

SIR CHARLES FIRTH: CROMWELL AND RELIGION IN THE ARMY [9]

The question of soldiers preaching was one of the subjects of
Cromwell's controversy with the Scottish clergy after the battle of
Dunbar [1650]. Cromwell invited the ministers who had taken
refuge in Edinburgh Castle to come down and preach freely in the
churches of the city. They declined, complaining that men of mere
civil place and employment should usurp the calling and employment of the ministry to the scandal of the Reformed Kirks, and
particularly in Scotland.

"Are you troubled that Christ is preached," replied Cromwell,
"Be not envious that Eldad and Medad prophesy. Where do you
find in the Scriptures a ground to warrant such an assertion that
preaching is exclusively your function?" Ordination, in his view,
was merely "an act of conveniency in respect of order."

In the end both Cromwell himself and the majority of the leaders

[9] C. H. Firth, *Cromwell's Army* (London: University Paperbacks, 1962), pp.
335–38. Reprinted by permission of Associated Book Publishers Ltd.

of the army seem to have come to the conclusion that some regulation of the right to preach was necessary in the interests of order and decency. On July 17, 1653 the Council of State, which the army had established after the expulsion of the Long Parliament, passed an order which was almost equivalent to the ordination of five officers named. It declared that "as the Council is satisfied of the gifts and abilities of Major Packer, Captain Empson, etc., and that the public exercise thereof will be of great use in the Church, they being eminent for godliness . . ." therefore the said persons "may have free use of any pulpit to preach in, as the Lord giveth opportunity," on the sole condition that the regular minister was not using it at the time.

It was to meet the case of Packer and other officers in his position that the Protector in 1657 persuaded Parliament to insert an amendment in the constitution known as the Petition and Advice. A clause in the original draft incapacitated public preachers from sitting in Parliament. Cromwell urged that the House should make it plain that it meant to exclude professionals only, "such as have the pastoral function," for otherwise many excellent officers would be excluded from Parliament.

"For I must say to you on behalf of our Army—in the next place to their fighting they have been very good preachers and I should be sorry they should be excluded from serving the Commonwealth, because they have been accustomed to preach to their troops, companies, and regiments—which I think has been one of the blessings upon them to the carrying on of the great work. There may be some of us, it may be, who have been a little guilty of that, who would be loath to be excluded from sitting in Parliament."

All this freedom of preaching and discussions and speculation naturally produced in the army beliefs of every conceivable variety and of every possible degree of extravagance. Yet there was no period at which this freedom was absolutely unlimited. Throughout the whole time there were certain opinions which no man could publicly profess without risking exclusion from the army. There were also certain religious sects whose members were gradually eliminated from the army not so much, however, for religious as for political reasons. By the operation of these two processes the character and temper of the army was very sensibly modified during the later years of its existence. Religious enthusiasm still worked powerfully amongst the soldiers, but it had come to adopt less extravagant forms. A sober Congregationalism became the dominant form of religion.

The elimination of the more extravagant religious sects took place mainly during the Protectorate, though it began during the Commonwealth. The rising of the Levellers in 1649 was a purely political and social movement, but since extreme opinions in religion and politics were generally associated, the result of the suppressions was that many of the wilder sectaries were driven out of the army.

It was to this no doubt that John Cotton referred when he congratulated Cromwell on "cashiering sundry corrupt spirits out of the army," though his letter was written nearly a couple of years after the rising. "Truly, Sir," he added, "better a few and faithful than many and unsound. The army on Christ's side (which he maketh victorious) are called chosen and faithful (Rev. xvii, 14), a verse worthy of your Lordship's frequent and deep meditation. Go on therefore, good Sir, to overcome yourself (Prov. xvi, 32), to overcome your army (Deut. xxix, 9 with v, 14), and to vindicate your orthodox integrity in the world."

The first important breach in the army which was primarily due to religious causes took place in 1654. The abdication of the Little Parliament [that is, the Assembly of Saints] put an end to the hopes which the Fifth Monarchy men had based upon its meeting, while the establishment of the Protectorate was a direct challenge to their most cherished principles. They had dreamed of a theocratic republic; they saw in its place a government which seemed to be the old monarchy in a new form. Cromwell, as they expressed it, had taken the crown from the head of Christ and put it on his own. From the moment of Cromwell's installation, therefore, Feake and Simpson and Rogers and other Fifth Monarchy preachers denounced the Protectorate and appealed to the army to overthrow it. "Lord," cried Vavasour Powell, "have our men all apostatized from their principles? What is become of all their declarations, protestations, and professions? Are they choked with lands, parks, and manors? Let us go home and pray, and say, "Lord, wilt thou have Oliver Cromwell or Jesus Christ to reign over us?" I know there are many gracious souls in the army, and of good principles, but the greater they grow the more they are corrupted with lands and honours." The Protector regarded the "Fifth Monarchy" as "a mistaken notion," by which many honest and sincere people had unhappily been misled. "A notion I hope we all honour, and wait and hope for: that Jesus Christ will have a time to set up his reign in our hearts; by subduing those corruptions and lusts and evils, that are there; which now reign more in the world than, I hope, in due time they shall do." But this reign of Christ, he argued, must be taken in a spiritual, not a literal sense. "Men could not be permitted to betitle themselves that they are the only men to rule kingdoms, govern nations, and give laws to people, and determine property and liberty and everything else, on such a pretension as this is." Yet, he concluded, as these misguided men had many of them good intentions, they should be treated with lenity. But they must live peaceably and refrain from active attempts to overthrow the government.

JOHN BUCHAN: OLIVER CROMWELL'S COURT [10]

Having become ruler of England and prince in all but name, Oliver's sturdy good sense made him resolved to keep up a state worthy of his dignity. He succeeded in combining the intimacies of family life with the splendour of a court—"a court of sin and vanity," its critic croaks, "and the more abominable because they had not yet quite cast away the name of God but profaned it by taking it in vain among them." It was indeed a curious mixture of pageantry and piety, but the blend was impressive, the velvet glove with the hardness of steel behind it, the silken mantle over armour. There were interminable sermons—three hours when John Howe preached—and multitudinous lengthy prayers, and there was always a psalm at the supper parties. There were fast days when a sabbath calm filled the palace. But the ceremonial occasions were managed high and disposedly, for, as his bitterest critics confessed, Oliver "had much natural greatness and well became the place he

---

[10] John Buchan, *Oliver Cromwell* (London: Hodder & Stoughton Ltd., 1934), pp. 513–15. Reprinted by permission of A. P. Watt & Son as literary agents to the Tweedsmuir Trustees and on behalf of Hodder & Stoughton Ltd.

had usurped." He had one hundred thousand pounds to spend annually on his household, and, though he gave away at least a third of this in charity, he used the remainder well. He had his scarlet-coated life-guards, and, apart from lackeys some fifty gentlemen about his person clad in uniforms of black and grey with silver trimmings. He kept a good table, and his guests could taste the first pineapples ever brought to England. His own diet was plain English fare with no foreign kickshaws, and his drink was a light wine or a very small ale.

His one indoor hobby was music. At Hampton Court he had two organs, and at Whitehall a variety of instruments. Whenever he gave a dinner, whether to foreign ambassadors or parliament men or members of Council, he had music played throughout the evening. He loved the human voice and had a taste for glees and part-songs, in which he took a share. For art he had respect, and he saved the Raphael cartoons for England, but he had little knowledge of it; his inclination seems to have been towards realism, for he bade Lely in painting his portrait reproduce all the roughnesses of his face.[11] There is no evidence that he read much, or indeed anything, beyond the Bible, but he had a kindness for men of letters and protected even those who opposed him, and he was a painstaking chancellor of Oxford.

To the end of his life he remained the countryman, and his happiest hours were spent in the long week-ends at Hampton Court, where he constructed fish-ponds and a warren. That was the sole relaxation permitted him, for the times were too critical to go far from London. The only game he played was bowls, but in field sports he had a most catholic taste. Hawking had been the amusement of his earlier days and he never lost his zest for it. Old, out-at-elbow cavalier falconers won his favour, and he did his best to entice away Whitelocke's servant who had good skill in hawks. But hawking demanded a freedom of movement and a leisure which he did not possess, and as Protector he had few opportunities for it beyond an occasional day on Hounslow Heath. So also with hunting, another pastime of his youth. Marvell speaks of

[11] This famous story repeated by Buchan is probably apocryphal. In the first place, there is no evidence that Cromwell ever sat for Lely; in the second place, Lely in his portrait did in fact gloss over one wart.

his delight
In horses fierce, wild deer, or armour bright.

His love of dun deer was famous, and Queen Christina of Sweden collected as a present for him a small herd of reindeer, which was unfortunately destroyed by wolves before it could be despatched to England. As Protector he had to confine his indulgence in the chase to the park at Hampton Court, where after dinner he would sometimes course a buck, and amaze foreign ambassadors by his bold jumping.

Horses were his abiding passion. He suppressed bear-baiting and cock-fighting because of their cruelty, but his prohibition of horse-racing was only local and temporary, and due solely to its political danger as an excuse for royalist meetings. The old cavalry leader was the best judge of a horse in England. There is no evidence that he raced himself, but his stud was his delight, and he laboured to improve the breed. We hear of his well-matched coach-teams—reddish-grey and snow-white—better, said rumour, than any king of England had ever possessed. The Golden Barb and Darley Arabian had their predecessors in his stables, and every English agent on the Mediterranean shores held a roving commission from the Protector. He bought barbs in Tripoli and rabs from Aleppo, for he had had enough of the heavy Flanders brand and knew that what the English stock wanted was the fineness of the East.

ERNEST BARKER: THE IDEA OF LIBERTY (1937) [12]

This is an extract from a lecture given at Hamburg in December, 1936, in which Ernest Barker rather surprisingly and, to my mind, foolishly, compared Cromwell with Hitler.

The sole and ultimate responsibility of Cromwell, and the great period of his life by which his achievement and significance must ultimately be judged, belong to the five and a half years which lie between eviction of Parliament in April, 1653 and his

[12] Ernest Barker, *Oliver Cromwell and the English People* (London: Cambridge University Press, 1937), pp. 39–46. Reprinted by permission of Cambridge University Press.

death in September, 1658. True, he had been the dynamic and driving force for at least half a dozen years earlier, in every crisis of events. If any man won the war against the Royalists it was he. If any man was responsible for the execution of the King, it was he. If any man left a mark upon Ireland—and a cruel mark at that— it was he. But the real test came when—the war won, the King dead, Ireland and Scotland reduced, and Parliament finally evicted —he and his army stood at last, face to face with the final burden of decision. Fighting was over: the time for the short, sharp shrift of the sword was gone: the time had come for facing an opposition in peace, and by the methods of peace. The opposition was numer- ous—far more numerous than the government—and though it was various and divided, its different sections were gradually beginning to coalesce. On the extreme Right stood the Royalists and Anglicans: on the moderate Right (but still on the Right) there were some who were Presbyterian Parliamentarians, and some who were plain Parliamentarians, clinging to the notion of a traditional and his- toric constitution of which an historic Parliament was a necessary and essential ingredient. The Right in general, which carried with it the instincts of the country, was the side of civilianism in the face of military rule: it was the side of traditionalism; it was also, because that was part of the tradition, the side of religious uni- formity. But there was also a Left, which went far beyond Cromwell and the main body of Independents. There were political Levellers, or Radicals, who had a passion for the sovereignty of the people, manhood suffrage, the natural rights of man, and the whole of the full-fledged doctrine of revolutionary democracy which emerged in France in 1789. There were also the social Levellers—men who would be called today Communists, but who confined their com- munism, as was natural in an agrarian age, to an attack on property in land, and to the assertion that "the Earth is the Lord's, not particular men's who claim a proper interest in it above others." The social Levellers were few; but in raising the issue of private property, and in pressing it against the general and captain of the Independent army, they brought out a fact which must not be forgotten. Cromwell and the men with whom he worked were themselves, in many respects, innovators and radicals. But on the point of property they too were traditional and conservative. The doctrine of the Free Churches did not entail any social programme, or any new distribution of property.

In face of this opposition Cromwell stood, first and foremost, as he had always stood, for religious liberty. He stood for the idea and practice of the Limited State which did not enforce religious uniformity, but was bound by the "fundamental" of respecting Christian freedom of conscience and Christian freedom of worship. This meant an ensured and guaranteed toleration, obligatory on the State, and superior to the State, which thus became, under the compulsion of an overriding principle of religious liberty, the home of various forms of belief living in a common peace and interacting on one another in a mutual influence.

But the toleration which was thus to proceed from the nature of a limited State was a toleration sadly and drastically limited in its own nature. Bound by the spirit of their own belief, which could only recognize as "true religion" the Protestant form of religion, and only the more Protestant form of that form, Cromwell and his associates in the Free Churches could not tolerate Anglicanism, and far less Roman Catholicism. Both Prelacy and Popery lay beyond the pale. This was a large and sweeping exception to the principle of religious liberty—so large and so sweeping that it may seem, at any rate to our own age, to negate the principle.

We have equally to remember that this principle, when it was enunciated, was a radical principle, and a flat contradiction of the current doctrine of the equivalence of people, commonwealth and church. The fundamental principle, in spite of the sad and drastic exceptions to its application, is that a man may freely celebrate his worship, according to the motion of his spirit, and that no earthly authority may interfere with that motion. Cromwell, like Luther, had a firm hold of the idea of the liberty of the Christian man in the inner springs of his life; and that idea carried him even farther than Luther, because it led him to deny, as Luther never did, the doctrine of religious territorialism—the doctrine of the equivalence of political and religious society. "Truly, these things do respect the souls of men, and the spirits, which are the men." "The mind is the man."

He stood for this idea in the first Civil War. "For brethren, in things of the mind," he had written to Parliament in 1645, "we look for no compulsion, but that of light and reason." He had stood for it in the second Civil War. "I desire from my heart," he wrote in 1648, "I have prayed for . . . union and right understanding between the godly people—Scots, English, Jews, Gentiles, Presbyterians, Anabaptists, and all." He stood for it still in the system he created in the days of his power and Protectorate. Religious funds and endowments were used for the common benefit of the Presbyterian clergy and Independent clergy of the Congregationalist and Baptist varieties. By the side of the clergy paid from these funds and endowments there also existed clergy, of whatever variety or denomination, supported by the free offerings of their own voluntary congregations. The Quakers were a notable example of such voluntary congregations; but the sects were numerous in these tumultuous times. Even the Anglicans sometimes met, illegally but by connivance, for public worship; and though even that was denied to the Roman Catholics, there was no other persecution of their belief, nor were they dragooned into attendance at alien forms of worship by fine and punishment, as had been the case under the previous law of England.

In this qualified form there was, under Cromwell, a brief summer of religious liberty—not improperly so called when we remember the period of compulsory religious uniformity which preceded it, and the similar period which followed it when King and Church and Parliament were restored in 1660. This summer had abiding fruits. Thanks to Cromwell, as one of his biographers has said, "Nonconformity had time to take root and to grow so strong in England that the storm which followed the Restoration had no power to root it up." English Nonconformity, with its doctrine of the limited State, and its aspiration towards a religious liberty which might become also a liberty in other spheres, continued to be a salt ingredient of English life, which maintained its peculiar savour and produced some of its most vital characteristics.

C. V. WEDGWOOD: "HE LOVED THE PEOPLE" (1939) [13]

Dame Wedgwood has expressed her views about Cromwell in various of her writings. In The King's War *(1958), she says that he "was melancholic, hypochrondiac, at times given to delusions" and that "he had found God by hard unaided wrestlings of the spirit and he believed with all the passion of his intense being that every man had a right and duty to find his own way to God." The following are the views she held thirty years ago.*

Much though not all of Cromwell's work died with him. His immediate service had been to stop the civil strife of England and give her back unity and self-respect. His more permanent service was to strengthen and develop the spirit of religious enquiry of individuals and the resistance to mental authority in the English, which flowered into the ineradicable, indestructible, harsh, fertile, stubborn growth of Nonconformity. His reforms might be swept away by the cross-currents and changes of the Restoration. Fundamentally the mark he had left on English history stayed for ever.

His body, buried with great pomp in the Abbey was disinterred two years later and hanged at Tyburn; the last fate of his bones has never been conclusively proved. They have long since mouldered into the earth of his native land.

Many different estimates of his moral character and his aspirations have been made. In his last years he had often spoken bitterly, calling the people "a many-headed beast, incapable of reason" and declaring that the sword alone was the best argument. Yet, casting up such statements against others of a more generous kind, it is easy to see that even to the end he hoped for some better foundation for his government than mere force. Intensely, tragically he loved the people and felt his responsibility towards them, nor did he ever wholly lose touch with them. To them his last thoughts turned; for them he prayed.

Even his last prayer shows how little he believed in force as a true basis for government. In the twilight of his consciousness he uttered the phrase which gives the key to all "consistency of judgment, one heart and mutual love"—the only foundation for the

[18] C. V. Wedgwood, *Oliver Cromwell*, pp. 139–41. Copyright © by C. V. Wedgwood, 1962, 1966. Reprinted by permission of The Macmillan Company and Gerald Duckworth & Co., Ltd.

permanent society. Dying, he could again be the idealist and the Christian that he had been before and, in all those years of stress, had vainly striven still to be.

The old story went on without end, his life but an incident in the unending sequence—force answered by force bringing full chaos, and chaos brought to order again by force. His career resolves itself into a statement of that problem which we today are once more called upon to solve. We need not here discuss the nature of civil liberty; it is always a limited and partial thing, as much in our time as in Cromwell's, though in different ways. Such as it was, Cromwell believed in it and fought for it. But while the war lasted liberty was at an end and when the wars were over the liberty of the victors became the oppression of the vanquished. The dominating power of the State changes its name, not its nature.

Yet against the worst of all disillusionments—the discovery that the thing saved was not the thing fought for—Cromwell had his answer. Even at moments of deep anxiety he kept that passionate belief in God which lends to his actions something at once fantastic and sublime. He never learnt the politicians' cynicism and he turned his back deliberately on the obvious truth that in the affairs of the world there is no right and wrong but only the expedient and the inexpedient. He was spared the humiliation of self-contempt which had he had a more acutely logical mind, he could not have avoided; for while he acted as circumstances dictated, he never ceased to believe that his doubtful compulsion was "none other than the hand of God."

ROBERT S. PAUL: "I WAS NOT DISOBEDIENT TO THE HEAVENLY VISION" (1955) [14]

To leave the description of his character without mentioning his religion would be to present the body without a soul. Oliver said of himself, "No man, no man, but a man mistaken and greatly mistaken, could think that I, that hath a burden upon my back for the space of fifteen or sixteen years—unless he would before-

[14] Robert S. Paul, *The Lord Protector* (London: Lutterworth Press, 1955), pp. 384–87. Reprinted by permission of the Lutterworth Press.

hand judge me an atheist—would seek such a place as I bear." And that is the issue: Cromwell's religion was either central to his life, or else he was a cynical unbeliever. No judicious historian could deny that within the Lord Protector's career, often hidden to himself, material considerations dissembled motives and lesser ends played their part; yet all through his life there is the consistent evidence of sincere personal religion and the influence of his theological and ecclesiastical concepts is too evident to be disregarded or explained away as merely the thought-forms of his day. They were the thought-forms of his day, but there was all Heaven and Hell behind them.

In 1656 the Venetian ambassador wrote of the Protector, "It cannot be denied that by his ability and industry he has contributed to his own greatness," but he added, "with all his abounding courage, good sense and natural prudence, all these qualities would have served him for nothing if circumstances had not opened the way to greatness." The Italian envoy perhaps would not have appreciated the religious significance of his own words, but it was in the amazing circumstances of his own career that Cromwell discerned and tested the validity of the divine call that he believed was his. That strict doctrine of Providence which held with John Calvin that "the righteous are the special objects of His favour, the wicked and profane the special objects of His severity" was not only the stimulus of Cromwell's single-minded purpose throughout the civil wars, and the foundation of his claim to a vocation of statesmanship, but during the vicissitudes of the Protectorate it was also the one sure anchor of hope that God would be with him to the end. It is possible to criticize this interpretation of Providence, or the exclusive view of "Election" and "Grace" in Calvinism, or the literal Biblicism and extravagant apocalyptic hopes of Puritanism, but however much these ideas may be criticized, they were factors, and often governing factors, in conditioning the life and thoughts of seventeenth-century England, and we disregard them only at the expense of misinterpreting the period.

In the same way it is possible to ridicule the idea of a troop of cavalry or Council of Army officers organized as a "gathered Church," but it was recognized by Richard Baxter after Naseby,

and that keen critic admitted the honesty of Cromwell's intention
when he said, "I conjecture, that at his first choosing such men into
his Troop, it was the very esteem and love of religious men that
principally moved him." Sir Ernest Barker has commented that
"the habit of the Independents was always a habit of congregationalism. Even the Independent army debated, because it was a congregation as well as an army." In Baxter's testimony, in the nature
of the Army Council and its discussions, and in the continuous
influence of the Army's opinion on Cromwell's own decisions, we
see these words were true not only in a general sense, but also in
the particular and personal sense of a man's relationship with his
"Church."

It is within this kind of setting that Oliver Cromwell saw his own
divinely appointed task on behalf of the people of England. He
was only accidentally—or "providentially"—a soldier and statesman, and he owned few political theories that could be regarded
as inviolable. It was "lawful" to pass through any form of Government for the accomplishing his ends and he reminded the Army
officers in 1647 that the Hebrews had experimented with several
different kinds of government. "If you should change the government to the best of it," he commented, "it is but, as Paul says,
'dross and dung in comparison of Christ' ": forms of government,
no less than individuals, were to be brought under the judgment
of the Biblical revelation, and the proof of divine approval was
to be sought in that "chain of Providence" by which nations and
individuals were led.

It might be thought at first that because Cromwell's sense of
vocation was based upon personal experience it therefore must have
been entirely subjective—an arbitrary declaration of his own purpose that brooked no argument or interference: "Come, come, I
will put an end to your prating . . . call them in, call them in!" A
closer study, however, will show that his sense of vocation is not
to be dismissed so summarily, for it was endorsed not only by the
actual sense of his undertakings but it was also tested by the Word
of Scripture. The importance of these factors can be seen when
Cromwell's career is compared with more modern dictators, for
whereas his conception of duty might lead him to act dictatorially,

it could never lead him to act amorally, much less contrary to Biblical morality in so far as he understood it: Cromwell might misinterpret the Biblical standards, he might be guilty of faulty exegesis, but he could never deliberately mishandle Scripture, for he had placed himself under the judgment of its revelation. Similarly with regard to the doctrine of Providence, he could not believe that God was with him, unless he could assure himself of a clean conscience; for, according to his own beliefs, his success was entirely due to the singleness of purpose with which he and his troops had tried to obey God's will. There may be occasions when we are able to discern beneath Oliver's passionate assertions of high calling the shape of less worthy motives, but he never gives any indication in private letter or public utterances that these motives were consciously recognized by him: Cromwell acted like a prophet, and the true prophet "is one who can say wih Paul, 'I was not disobedient to the heavenly vision.' "

Throughout his public life we see the future Lord Protector struggling to reconcile these fundamental convictions first with the military and political needs of the nation, secondly with his own responsibility within the nation, and finally with the position of the English Protectorate within the context of world affairs. Perhaps the way in which he met the circumstances of his time on the basis of his professed beliefs tell us more about his character than any summary of his personal attributes.

A. H. WOOLRYCH: "GREATNESS OF HEART" (1964) [15]

Austin Woolrych is Professor of Modern History at the University of Lancaster and author of Battles of the English Civil War.

We cannot simply write off Cromwell's career as a failure because his cause fell in ruins at the Restoration. The English Revolution of 1640–1660 was not simply a violent interlude in Britain's

---

[15] A. H. Woolrych, *Oliver Cromwell* (Oxford: The Clarendon Press, 1964), pp. 56–8, 59. Reprinted by permission of The Clarendon Press.

history, but a crucial turning point which has affected its whole course since then. . . . Though he would have regarded the Restoration as a disaster, much that he strove for was accomplished, at least in part, after his time: toleration in 1689, the working out from then on of a balanced constitution, union with Scotland in 1707, the gradual reform of the law, even the growth of new universities —for one of the many works for education (reversed, alas, at the Restoration) was the founding of a university college at Durham.

His character was neither small nor simple. To sum it up in two or three pages is like taking as many minutes to explore a vast, crowded painting by the light of a feeble torch—a painting, at that, of which parts have crumbled away with time, or been daubed over.

It is perhaps easiest to assess him as a soldier, for as such his greatness is unquestionable. We cannot judge him beside (say) Marlborough or Napoleon, because the scale of his wars was much smaller, and their tactics and strategy more limited. But within these limits he developed skill of a high order—and he was forty-three before he first drew his sword. Moreover, it was a moral ascendancy, no less than military skill, which enabled him to lead to victory those soldiers who "knew what they fought for and loved what they knew."

As a statesman he is harder to judge. His enemies held the view that he plotted cunning traps for his opponents, and by deluding or discrediting them raised himself stage by stage to supreme power. No serious historian holds that view today. Indeed, he seldom saw far ahead; he was more apt to wait upon events than to shape them deliberately. He usually responded to a difficult political situation by going through weeks of troubled indecision (in contrast with the swift energy of his military campaigns) before finally emerging in some sharp burst of action. The critical decisions of his career—to attack the *conduct* of the war in 1644, to join the army's revolt in 1647, to bring Charles I to trial, to expel the Rump, to accept the Protectorate, to refuse the crown—were not taken swiftly, or without first searching painfully for some easier way out. And when he did act it was generally along lines to which others had been pointing for some time. For in politics he was no great originator; one can trace at different stages the strong influence on him of Vane, Ireton, Harrison, and Lambert, among others. This was not necessarily weakness, though he was not a born politician in the way that he was a born soldier. His apparent lack of farsightedness sprang partly from his faith as a Puritan. Since everything that happened was ordained by Divine Providence, a conviction grew on him with his victories that he was the humble instrument of God's purpose for England. He never claimed that God spoke to him directly, as some more fanatical Puritan "saints" did. But in every situation, and in nearly all his speeches, he searched the shape of recent events for "providences," "dispensations," "appearances of God" that might show him how he was meant to act next. He would lay no deep plans for the further future; the next move but one, or two, or three, was God's business, not man's. This was, of course, a dangerous creed for a man of Cromwell's power; it could mean that God was on the side of whoever had won the last battle—that might was right, in fact. He was aware of the temptation to "make too much of outward dispensations," and to mistake "fleshly reasonings" and "carnal imagination" for the will of God. But it was a temptation that he did not always avoid.

This waiting upon Providence explains much that may seem inconsistent in his career—why he supported first a limited monarchy, then a republic, next an assembly of "saints," and finally, in the Protectorate, a sort of limited monarchy again. To the exasperation of the Levellers, republicans, and others, he declared that all forms of government "might be good in themselves, or for us, according as providence should direct us." But if the means he used seem inconsistent, there were certain basic aims that he pursued throughout his career. These aims he would sum up as "our civil and religious liberties"—"our civil liberties as men, our spiritual liberties as Christians." With regard to religious liberty he was ahead of his time, and ahead of most of his fellow Puritans, in his passionate conviction that men come to the truth by different ways, and that only evil could result from forcing their consciences.

In the matter of civil liberties his record is more chequered. He believed sincerely in the rule of law, in getting things done by discussion and consent rather than by force, and in the people's right to be governed under laws made by their representatives. Yet he quarrelled with one Parliament after another. When his aims clashed with theirs, they had to go; but it was not because their aims were more liberal than his that he broke with them. He cared strongly for justice, and interfered as little with the courts of law as the safety of his government allowed. Despite constant plotting against the Protectorate remarkably few men suffered death for it, and few political prisoners languished in his gaols. Some he held for a time without trial because he did not want to charge them with treason, which carried the death penalty; and some of these were imprisoned only after he had tried, in long and patient interviews, to persuade them to give their word not to act against the government. For a revolutionary regime, he was notably mild, and to liken it to a modern police state is absurd. As the Royalist Earl of Clarendon acknowledged, he was "not a man of blood." . . .

If his mind was austere, it was never mean. We must not close our eyes to those "roughnesses, pimples, warts, and everything," which he himself told Sir Peter Lely to paint when he sat for his portrait. But when all is said, we may still find in him a greatness of heart that makes our history the richer for his stormy passage through it.

HUGH TREVOR-ROPER: CROMWELL'S "SOCIAL REVOLUTION" (1967) [16]

Hugh Trevor-Roper is one of a number of modern historians who lay stress upon the importance of social structure or class in the development of past events. His ideas about the "declining gentry" in seventeenth-century England have stimulated a considerable number of investigators on both sides of the Atlantic. According to Trevor-Roper's view, Cromwell belonged to the declining gentry who resented the wealth of the courtiers. Unfortunately, his views about Cromwell lie scattered among his published writings. I quote here from his latest collection of essays.

[16] Hugh Trevor-Roper, *Religion, the Reformation and Social Change* (London: Macmillan & Co., Ltd., 1967), pp. 412–13, 415, 416–17. Reprinted by permission of Macmillan & Co., Ltd., and A. D. Peters & Co.

What was the nature of the social revolution which Cromwell sought to export to Scotland? In England that revolution was not essentially radical, though it had needed radical methods for its achievement. Essentially it was a seizure of power in the state by the classes who had been accustomed to power in the country but who, under the Stuarts, had been, or had felt themselves more and more excluded by a parasitic Court and its Church: in other words, by the laity, the gentry. In opposition these men had demanded, and now in power they sought to realize, a general policy of decentralization and laicization. The feudal taxes, the antique patronage which had sustained the Court and its peerage were to be abolished, together with the Court and the House of Peers: the Parliament was to be reduced to a parliament of gentry, and country gentry at that—the reduction of borough seats and the multiplication of county seats would achieve that purpose. Education was to be decentralized by the foundation of new local schools and colleges, laicized by the reform of teaching and the adoption of new "Baconian" subjects. Religion was to be decentralized by the break-up of episcopal and capitular property, the redistribution of patronage, and the use of both for the "propagation of the Gospel" in remote, neglected areas. At the same time it was to be laicized by practical lay control and systematic toleration. Law was to be decentralized by breaking the monopoly of the London law courts and setting up "county registers" and "county judicatories" and laicized by the simplification of procedure and language. The whole policy was summarized as "reformation of law and clergy."

Of course there were differences of interpretation. Some men interpreted the policy in a conservative, some in a radical even a revolutionary spirit. Oliver Cromwell himself interpreted it in a conservative spirit. He believed that the policy should be carried out by the gentry. But equally he insisted that its benefits must be enjoyed by those humbler allies whose voices, in the counties and more democratic boroughs, had carried the Puritan gentry into Parliament in 1640 and whose arms, in the New Model Army, had since carried them through radicalism to power. All his life Cromwell would never betray "the godly party"—that is, the country party in depth, the alliance of gentle and simple which alone could preserve the gains of revolution—and many of his apparent inconsistencies, from his surrender to the Agitators in 1647 to his rejection of the crown in 1657, are to be explained by this genuine resolve never to betray his followers or to split the "godly party." . . .

The parallel between Cromwell's policy in Scotland and in England can be seen, first of all, in the character of his advisers. If we wish to see the continuity and consistency of his English policy, we can look at the group of civilians whom he kept around him. These men, who were his ablest supporters in his nominated Parliament, the Barebones Parliament,[17] and who continued with him in the Council of State of the Protectorate, are first found in this group, significantly enough, in that committee for the reform of the law which Cromwell personally forced the Rump Parliament to set up in 1652. These three, with one addition, reappear as the nominated Scottish Members of the Barebones Parliament; and they continue as Scottish members of the Scottish Council of State. In their common origin, as well as their diverse past, these men illustrate both the consistent aim and the conciliatory method of Cromwell's policy.

These were the Scotsmen with whose aid Cromwell sought to carry the English social revolution, as he understood it, into Scotland: a revolution, there too, of "reformation of law and clergy." And what did this mean in fact, in Scottish circumstances? First of all, it meant reducing the power of those who, in civil wars, in Scotland as in England, had frustrated the expression and application of such a policy: that is, of the great lords, with their oppressive patronage and the intolerant Kirk, with its monopoly of the pulpit. It was the union of these two forces which had first launched the National Covenant and so made the English Revolution possible; but by now the same forces were the main obstacle to the progress of that revolution in their own land, and as such they must be broken. The English Commonwealth was determined to set up in Scotland, as in England, a gentry-republic, where all land was free of feudal burdens, where the patronage of the nobility

---

[17] The "Barebones Parliament" generally is referred to elsewhere in this book as the Assembly of Saints; it also is sometimes called the Little Parliament.

was destroyed, and where the Church had no coercive power over the laity. "Free the poor commoners," was the cry of hopeful Scots after the battle of Worcester "and make as little use as can be either of the great men or clergy."

Afterword

Those who have read carefully through the three parts of this book will, I believe, be left with strikingly different impressions about what Cromwell himself regarded as important in his life, about how his contemporaries judged him, and about how historians have measured him. With Cromwell himself we see an almost desperate groping after truth and justice, order and liberty. He was constantly perplexed over what was right or wrong in political decisions and tried to determine from events—the dispensations of the Almighty—the path he ought to follow. Historians tend to assess statesmen according to some pattern of principle (whether that is their task is another question), but statesmen themselves are confronted with many completely unexpected problems that they have to solve with a fair degree of rapidity, not always according to principle, but according to the pressing necessities of the moment.

I once asked a friend of mine, who had passed much of his career as a high civil servant in the British Treasury, which of the Chancellors of the Exchequer he had served under he had most admired. A little to my surprise, he said Harold Macmillan. When I asked him why, he replied that Macmillan was the only leading Minister who had been apt to think in terms of the years that lay ahead. Most statesmen, he averred, were content to think in terms, at most, of three months ahead and often, merely in terms of the reactions that might be expected from the world they governed, next week. Cromwell, it is often remarked by those who have studied him most closely, was slow in making up his mind. Often, he was faced with an accomplished fact—such as Cornet Joyce's seizure of the King's person at Holmby House or the "purge" of the House of Commons by Colonel Pride. In both these cases, the evidence suggests that Cromwell tried to modify the consequences of such drastic actions, and in his life he often appears in the role of a conciliator, of a man who was genuinely trying to appreciate the difficulties of his opponents or his colleagues.

But at the same time, he was a man in authority. He thought that his authority had been thrust upon him, that even if reluctantly, he had become in duty bound the chosen leader of a chosen people. So, at any rate after 1652, he was highly conscious that he had been called upon to impose law and order upon a land torn by ten years of civil wars. Hence he groped, as most statesmen have groped—especially in times of war or civil strife—at a position somewhere between upholding the principles of individual liberty as far as was possible and maintaining a reasonably stable system of government. In our own times, we have seen leading statesmen such as, say, Presidents Franklin D. Roosevelt and Lyndon B. Johnson, in the United States, and Sir Anthony Eden and President Charles De Gaulle, in Europe, confronted with this type of situation.

It is easy for historians, looking backward, to argue that such statesmen have been inconsistent in their policies or have been untrue to their principles or have violated invaluable individual freedoms by using the state's power on wrong occasions. In fact, most statesmen are fully aware of the dangers of applying force to maintain order—and certainly Cromwell was conscious of that. Few people today, I imagine, would fancy that racial problems in mixed communities or economic problems in long-established capitalist societies, where wage earners demand a larger share of the national income, can be resolved permanently simply by forceful action on the part of the government. Thus Cromwell tried to reconcile his opponents, to promote agreed reforms, to allow as much liberty of conscience as he could without undermining the very fabric of society.

Similarly, inconsistencies may be detected in his attitude toward foreign affairs. He was awake, for example, to the value of the cloth export industry to England's prosperity and was anxious to maintain the freedom of the seas for British commerce, particularly in the Baltic and in the Mediterranean. Yet at the same time, he was aware of a duty to international Protestantism. He undoubtedly feared—probably anachronistically—that the two Hapsburg monarchs, who ruled in Madrid and Vienna, but who had in fact been exhausted by interminable wars, would combine to impose another Counter-Reformation on Europe by force of arms. He therefore pictured the King of Sweden and the leaders of the Dutch Republic as allies whom he ought to sustain. He came to terms with the neighboring government of France because it obviously was a foe of the Hapsburgs. Understandably, he was disappointed when he discovered that the Swedes and the Dutch had other, more material interests—though in fact, the English had material interests too, which Cromwell recognized; and Cromwell's right-hand man, John Lambert, was ready to seek an alliance with the Spaniards simply because they were valuable customers for British goods.

In Cromwell, therefore, we perceive an earnest and painful striving after solutions to difficult political problems, which is a habit characteristic of all leading statesmen. And we see how often his broader ideals were hampered, vitiated, or confused by the day-to-day facts of government.

If we turn to the outlook of his contemporaries, we are struck by some measure of agreement over what was felt about him by his friends and his enemies. A word that frequently was applied to him is *magnanimity*. By this was meant not so much what we would mean by the word today—that is, a kind of large-minded tolerance—but rather a strength of will and character that obviously impressed anybody who associated with him. "If the chief should die," wrote the Venetian Resident, then neither his sons nor anyone else would be capable of replacing him. Mrs. Hutchinson, who disliked Cromwell, admitted the contrast between him and the other officials of the Protectorate government. He was, said some, "gallant, great and magnanimous"; he showed "magnanimous resolution" in his enterprises. Two achievements appear to have impressed his contemporaries most. First, there was the spirit he inspired in his soldiers: "he first put arms into Religion's hand," wrote the poet. Richard Baxter also bore testimony to the unique character of Cromwell's army, which has been carefully delineated for us by Sir Charles Firth. Secondly, his contemporaries referred almost unanimously to the power and prestige he acquired outside his own country. Again, a poet summarizes this precisely, when he writes that "he made us freeman of the Continent," while Cromwell's critic, the Earl of Clarendon, observes that "his greatness at home was but a shadow of the glory he had abroad." It is facile to say that Charles I—or Henry VIII—was the true founder of the British navy and that it was a fortuitous consequence of the long civil war that Cromwell had at his disposal, during his Protectorate, a well-trained standing army that he could send on expeditions overseas. Here it is interesting to observe a pretty sharp contrast between the opinions of contemporaries and those of later historians. David Hume wrote, for example, that Cromwell's "foreign enterprises" were "pernicious to the national interests," and later historians have asserted that he could never make up his mind whether he was a Protestant crusader or a commercial traveler. Achievement in foreign policy is extremely hard to gauge. But if its aim is to create admiration and fear among one's neighbors, it was certainly recognized at the time that Cromwell had attained that position for the British Commonwealth: and this was avowed by one of the greatest of his contemporaries, Cardinal Mazarin.

Turning now to "Cromwell in history," it is clear that the dividing line in historiography occurred in the middle of the nineteenth century, when Thomas Carlyle edited Cromwell's letters and speeches. In the eighteenth century, Cromwell had been regarded, on the whole, as a hypocrite and a fanatic, though these are obviously contradictory terms. Some historians have thought, with Gardiner, that "the man was greater than his work." Others have felt that no Englishman has done more to shape the future of the land that he governed.

Possibly what all this boils down to in the end is the view that one takes of the individual's place in history. Should we believe that it would have made no difference to the history of France whether Napoleon, or Moreau, emerged as her leader; or whether, say, Mendes-France had taken the place of De Gaulle in the Fifth Republic? The modern scientific historian, who has been remarkably influenced by the teachings of Karl Marx, is inclined to analyze historical events in the light of social structure and class war. On this kind of reckoning, Cromwell was the agent of a specific social class. He was out, as Hugh Trevor-Roper argues, to overthrow the established nobility and the grandees of the Church of England or Kirk of Scotland and create a "gentry-republic." Or as Christopher Hill might express it, he was the unwilling agent of a great revolution. Earlier historians like Sir Ernest Barker would regard Cromwell rather as the precursor of the limited and liberal state, who as far as he could consistently with the need to maintain law and order, stood for the freedom of the mind in all its forms. But what recent historians do appear to agree about—as I indicated in my introduction to this book—is that Cromwell was fundamentally a tolerant and conciliatory statesman, far removed from the police-state autocrats of more modern times.

History is no exact science, and everyone must look at Cromwell from his own point of view. But that his was a "great life" is hard to deny.

Bibliographical Note

There are two full collections of Cromwell's letters and speeches, though neither is entirely satisfactory or easily obtainable: *The Letters and Speeches of Oliver Cromwell: with Elucidations by Thomas Carlyle,* edited in three volumes by S. C. Lomas (London, 1904); and *The Writings and Speeches of Oliver Cromwell,* with an introduction, notes, and an account of his life by Wilbur Cortez Abbott, in four volumes (Cambridge: Harvard University Press, 1947). The latter contains a number of documents not in Lomas, but most of these are not of much significance. Abbott also edited a *Bibliography of Oliver Cromwell* (Harvard University Press, 1929), which is brought down to 1944 in the fourth volume of *The Writings and Speeches* as "Addenda to Bibliography" and which also was privately printed. Many of the items in these two bibliographies have little or no direct concern with Oliver Cromwell and include pamphlets and flysheets published in his lifetime. A select list of books published about Oliver Cromwell and include pamphlets and flysheets published in *The Greatness of Oliver Cromwell* (New York: Collier Books, 1962, 1966), and a select bibliography appears in Robert S. Paul, *The Lord Protector* (London, 1955). P. H. Hardacre discusses "Writings on Oliver Cromwell since 1929" in Vol. XXX of the *Journal of Modern History.* A selection of Cromwell's more important writings and of extracts from his speeches will be found in L. C. Bennett, *Letters and Speeches of Oliver Cromwell* (London, 1941). And a selection of views about Cromwell by historians and others is published in D. C. Heath's Problems of European Civilization series, edited by Richard E. Boyer, first published in New York in 1966 under the title *Oliver Cromwell and the Puritan Revolt: Failure of a Man or a Faith?*

171

Apart from books quoted in the text, Sir Charles Firth wrote a biography of Oliver Cromwell that was first published in Putnam's Heroes of the Nations series in 1901 and has been frequently republished since, in England by the Oxford University Press. Some people think that this is the best biography of Cromwell; the facts are reliable, the interpretation careful. Besides his book on Oliver Cromwell, originally published in 1899, Samuel Rawson Gardiner wrote in 1897 a book entitled *Cromwell's Place in History*. The *Oliver Cromwell* was reprinted as a paperback by Collier Books, with a new introduction by Maurice Ashley, in 1962. Maurice Ashley, *Oliver Cromwell and the Puritan Revolution*, first published in London by the English Universities Press in 1958, also is available as a paperback from Collier Books (New York), as is C. V. Wedgwood's *Oliver Cromwell*, a brief life. The English Historical Association published in 1958 a pamphlet about Oliver Cromwell by Dr. Christopher Hill that gives a kind of Marxist interpretation of his career. Besides A. H. Woolrych's book in the Clarendon series, there is another recent short biography, by Brigadier Peter Young (London: Batsford, 1963).

For the general background of Cromwell's life, there are the series of volumes written by Gardiner and Firth entitled *The History of the Great Civil War, The Commonwealth and Protectorate*, and *The Last Years of the Protectorate* (1886–1909), and *The Great Rebellion* by C. V. Wedgwood (1955, 1958), not yet completed. A recent book covering most of this ground has been written by Ivan Roots (London: Batsford, 1966); it is entitled *The Great Rebellion, 1642–1660*. It has a useful bibliography.

There are biographies of Cromwell in several other languages—for example, by the Italian writer E. Momigliano, translated into English in 1932, and one by W. Michael, in German (Berlin, 1907). Eduard Bernstein's *Cromwell and Communism*, a highly misleading title, was translated into English in 1930 and reprinted by Frank Cass in 1963. But most of these books either are superficial or have been superseded by later research. A stimulating recent essay is "Oliver Cromwell and his Parliaments," by Hugh Trevor-Roper, first published in 1956, the latest version of which will be found in his *Religion, The Reformation and Social Change* (London, 1967).

For Cromwell's military career, reference should be made to C. V. Wedgwood, *The King's War* (1958), A. H. Woolrych, *Battles of the Civil War* (London, 1961), and A. H. Burn and Peter Young, *The Great Civil War, 1642–1646: A Military History of the First Civil War* (London, 1959). Among older books are Maurice Ashley, *Cromwell's Generals* (1954); C. E. Lucas Phillips, *Cromwell's Captains* (1938); and T. S. Baldock, *Cromwell as a Soldier* (1899). An important recent addition to studies of Cromwell's foreign policy is Michael Roberts, "Cromwell and the Baltic," in *Essays in Swedish History* (London, 1967).

Views about whether the Independents really were Independents and the Presbyterians really were Presbyterians in Cromwell's day will be found scattered in articles in many learned journals, English and American: see also Ivan Roots, *op. cit.,* and George Yule, *The Independents in the English Civil War* (Cambridge, 1958).

Index

GREAT LIVES OBSERVED

Gerald Emanuel Stearn, *General Editor*

Other volumes in the series: